Reach
HIGHER

Program Authors

Nancy Frey

Lada Kratky

Nonie K. Lesaux

Sylvia Linan-Thompson

Deborah J. Short

Jennifer D. Turner

NATIONAL GEOGRAPHIC
LEARNING

Australia · Brazil · Mexico · Singapore · United Kingdom · United States

**NATIONAL
GEOGRAPHIC**
LEARNING

National Geographic Learning,
a Cengage Company

Reach Higher 6A
**Program Authors: Nancy Frey, Lada Kratky,
Nonie K. Lesaux, Sylvia Linan-Thompson,
Deborah J. Short, Jennifer D. Turner**

Publisher, English Medium Instruction (EMI):
   Erik Gundersen

Associate Director, R&D: Barnaby Pelter

Senior Development Editors:
   Jacqueline Eu
   Ranjini Fonseka
   Kelsey Zhang

Director of Global Marketing: Ian Martin

Heads of Regional Marketing:
   Charlotte Ellis (Europe, Middle East and Africa)
   Kiel Hamm (Asia)
   Irina Pereyra (Latin America)

Product Marketing Manager: David Spain

Senior Production Controller: Tan Jin Hock

Senior Media Researcher (Covers): Leila Hishmeh

Senior Designer: Lisa Trager

Director, Operations: Jason Seigel

Operations Support:
   Rebecca Barbush
   Drew Robertson
   Caroline Stephenson
   Nicholas Yeaton

Manufacturing Planner: Mary Beth Hennebury

Publishing Consultancy and Composition:
   MPS North America LLC

For permission to use material from this text or product,
submit all requests online at **cengage.com/permissions**
Further permissions questions can be emailed to
permissionrequest@cengage.com

ISBN-13: 978-0-357-36705-6

National Geographic Learning
20 Channel Center Street
Boston, MA 02210
USA

Locate your local office at **international.cengage.com/region**

Visit National Geographic Learning online at **ELTNGL.com**
Visit our corporate website at **www.cengage.com**

Printed in China
Print Number: 06   Print Year: 2023

Contents at a Glance

Table of Contents

The Power of Choice

Unit 1

Table of Contents

Survival

? BIG QUESTION
What does it take to survive?

SCIENCE
▸ Understanding Adaptations
▸ Survival

Table of Contents

Digging Up the Past

Unit 3

Table of Contents

Our Diverse Earth

Unit 4

? BIG QUESTION

Why is diversity important?

SCIENCE
▸ Ecosystems
▸ Conservation

Genres at a Glance

Unit 1

THE POWER OF CHOICE

BIG Question

How do choices affect who you are?

CHILEAN PATAGONIA, CHILE
A girl pushing her bike along Llanquihue Lake

Share What You Know

❶ **Read** this quotation:
"It is our choices . . . that show what we truly are, far more than our abilities."
– J.K. Rowling

❷ **Think** about choices.

❸ **Discuss** how choices make a difference.

Give Information

Listen to the information given in the poem. Then use **Language Frames** to give information about facing fear.

Language Frames

- _____ is _____ .
- When _____ , we _____ .
- If _____ , we _____ .
- One important detail is _____ .

Facing Fear 🔊

There is something about fear that traps us,
That stops and freezes our heart and our brain.
There is something in the air of dread
That is dark and doesn't let us breathe.

But when light shines over that fear
And lets us see the true nature of that thing,
The blindfold falls; the freezing stops,
And we can fly away without a single string.

Social Studies Vocabulary

Key Words

Key Words
capable
encounter
figure out
reputation
resistance

🔊 Key Words

Study the photos and captions. Use **Key Words** and other words to talk about the choices people with disabilities must make.

◀ People with disabilities may **encounter** certain difficulties, as communities often focus on the majority and overlook special needs. They have to **figure out** ways to overcome obstacles. Some blind people use their fingers to read books in braille.

▶ Many people with disabilities are perfectly **capable** of doing things we might not expect them to do. They may show **resistance** to getting help and not want to have a **reputation** for being dependent. However, sometimes they rely on friends or strangers.

Talk Together

What problems do some people with disabilities face? How could their choices affect their lives? Use **Language Frames** from page 4 and **Key Words** to discuss these questions and give information about the topic.

5

Main Idea

As you read about a topic, identify important details that the author repeats or explains. Then put the details together to help you figure out the **main idea**, or most important idea, of the text.

. . . Louis managed to finish the first years of basic education as a **notable scholar** and a **musician** as well. His **intelligence, dedication,** and **determination to learn** led him to obtain a scholarship . . .

"These **details** from the text tell some of Louis's qualities."

Map and Talk

A main idea diagram can help you keep track of important details as you read. After you finish reading, use the details to determine the main idea of the entire selection.

Main Idea Diagram

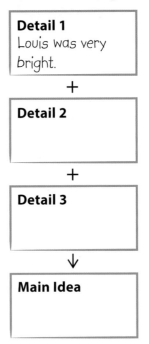

Detail 1
Louis was very bright.

+

Detail 2

+

Detail 3

↓

Main Idea

Interview a partner about an important choice he or she has made. Use a main idea diagram to keep track of the main idea and the supporting details.

🔊 More Key Words

Use these words to talk about "The Vision of the Sightless" and "A Work in Progress."

assumption
noun

An **assumption** is something that is believed to be true. When the dog wagged its tail, the boy made the **assumption** that the dog was friendly.

diverge
verb

When two things or ideas **diverge**, they differ or move away from each other. This hiking trail has two paths that **diverge** in different directions.

exclude
verb

When you **exclude** something, you leave it out. I **exclude** nuts from the recipe because I am allergic to them.

optional
adjective

Something that is **optional** is not needed or required. At our school, learning to play an instrument is an **optional** activity that you can choose.

potential
noun

Potential is the ability to change or improve in the future. The kids have **potential** to become great basketball players one day.

Talk Together

Work with a partner. Make a Word Web of examples for each **Key Word**.

weekend
sports   dessert

optional

extra credit   vacation
assignments   trips

Reading Strategy

Learn to Preview and Predict

Do you look through a book to see what it is like before you read it? If you do, you use the first step of a good reading strategy. Active readers **preview** a text before they read. As they read, they **predict**, or guess, what will happen next in the text.

How to Preview and Predict

1. Preview the text. Read the title. Then look at the pictures, text, and graphic features. Skim the first few paragraphs. What do you think this text is about?

The text is about _____.

2. As you read, use details to predict, or guess, what will come next in the text.

I read _____, and so I predict that _____.

3. Read on to confirm, or check, your prediction. As you learn more details, you may need to revise a prediction or make a new one.

My prediction was _____. Now, I predict _____.

Here's how one student made a prediction.

Look Into the Text

Louis found the new way of learning interesting and challenging, and he always showed a good disposition, doing what was required of him in the new school. However, he realized **this method of accessing information was very hard to figure out**, for him as well as for most of the other students. For that same reason, most of the classes he took involved teachers reading to the students.

"The text is about the **topic** of learning at the new school."

"I read **details** about how difficult learning was for the children, and so I predict that a solution will be proposed. I will read on to check or change my prediction."

Previewing a text and making predictions about what will happen next can make your reading more fun. It can also help you better understand and remember what you read.

Read the biographical profile and sample notes. Use **Language Frames** to tell a partner about your predictions.

Profile

Challenges
FOR A GENIUS

Ray Charles, a renowned and creative musician who shaped soul music, was born on September 23, 1930, in Albany, Georgia. As a little boy, he demonstrated an extraordinary ability for music, and he could play piano by the age of five. However, life was not going to be easy for this little genius.

When he was six years old, he started losing his sight gradually, becoming completely blind by the age of seven. His mother took care of him but was never overprotective. She soon made it clear to Ray that studying was not **optional** and that he should not feel sorry for himself, reminding him often that the loss of sight did not mean a loss of intelligence or will. She constantly encouraged her son to do what other children could do so that he did not feel **excluded**. While Ray's disability may have caused his life to **diverge**, it certainly did not hold him back. ◀

His studies at the Florida School for the Deaf and the Blind were crucial in the development of his **potential** as a musician. There, he perfected his piano technique and learned to play other instruments, such as the saxophone and the clarinet. More importantly, by learning to read and write in braille, he was able to start writing his own music. ◀

Ray lost his father at age 10 and then his mother at age 15. After his mother's passing, he left school to **figure out** his future, working with different music bands. He was a pianist, singer, composer, and band leader who always showed amazing energy in his work, self-confidence in everything he did, and incredible attention to detail in his performances. ◀

In spite of the many challenges he faced early in his life, Ray Charles was **capable** of not only becoming a successful musician with a **reputation** as "the only true genius in show business," but also a true humanitarian who supported others so that racial, physical, political, or economic barriers could not stop creative spirits.

The text is about a man named Ray Charles.

I read the title, and so I predict that the text will tell me about problems Ray Charles had to face.

My prediction was correct because the profile tells how Ray Charles lost his sight. Now, I predict he will show others how being blind is not always a limitation.

◀ = a good place to stop and make a prediction

Read a Biography

Genre

A **biography** is nonfiction. It is the story of a person's life, written by another person. The author of a biography shares information about someone else's life. "The Vision of The Sightless" was written by Laura A. Siqueiros, and she tells about Louis Braille's life, choosing the most relevant and interesting events to make his story attractive to others.

Point of View

Point of view describes how a story is told. The author of a biography writes in the **third-person point of view** and uses words such as the name of the person and *he* and *him* to tell the story.

> **Louis** was always positive and cheerful. **He** made good friends at the school and enjoyed activities prepared for students, such as visits to the botanical gardens in Paris. There were also music lessons, in which **he** continued to excel, and workshops where students like **him** would learn to make slippers or baskets.

🔊 THE VISION OF THE SIGHTLESS

By Laura A. Siqueiros

If we look carefully, we realize there are things to learn from each and every person around us. There are also many things to learn from the stories of people who did not live in our time but whose **legacy** is there to remind us that the **potential** of the human spirit knows no boundaries. Where some of us may see problems or limitations, others are able to view a situation as a challenge for which multiple solutions are possible. There are extraordinary people who, in the face of challenge, have been able to **diverge** in a new direction and create a solution not only for themselves but also for others. This is the case for Louis, who, after a tragic accident at a very young age, may have lost his sight but did not lose his vision.

Louis was born on January 4, 1809, in a small and peaceful town in France called Coupvray, which is near Paris. He was the youngest of four children. His father, Simon René, had a harness shop. Simon René was known in the town for making equipment to harness and control horses. To work with leather and other materials in his shop, Louis's father had a lot of tools, some of them sharp and dangerous. Little Louis was only three years old when he took one to play with and hurt his right eye in a very serious way. Louis was taken to the doctor right away, but his eye could not be saved. Moreover, he developed a rare condition that affected his second eye as well. By the age of five, Louis had become completely blind.

legacy gift passed on to future generations

Louis Braille

IN THIS HOUSE
ON JANUARY 4 1809
WAS BORN
Louis BRAILLE
THE INVENTOR OF THE SYSTEM OF
WRITING IN RAISED DOTS FOR USE
BY THE BLIND
HE OPENED THE DOORS OF
KNOWLEDGE TO ALL THOSE
WHO CANNOT SEE

▲ Louis Braille's childhood home

Louis's parents were determined that they would not allow their young son's life to be ruined by this horrible **misfortune**. They wanted him to have a full and independent life, and this demanded a solid education. Louis started going to school, where he learned by listening to his teachers. Life was not easy, but Louis managed to finish the first years of basic education as a **notable scholar** and a musician as well. His intelligence, dedication, and determination to learn led him to obtain a scholarship to attend the National Institute for Blind Children in Paris in 1819, when he was only 10 years old. The family's **assumption** was that the **prestigious** school would give Louis the opportunity to realize his full **potential**, and they were not mistaken.

At the school for the blind, young Louis started learning with the materials available at the time, which consisted mainly of books with raised letters and numbers that blind students had to recognize by touch. Louis found the new way of learning interesting and challenging, and he always showed a **good disposition**, doing what was required of him in the new school. However, he realized this method of accessing information was very hard to **figure out**, for him as well as for most of the other students. For that same reason, most of the classes he took involved teachers reading to the students.

▲ **Institut National des Jeunes Aveugles, in Paris, was the first special school for blind students in the world, and it served as a model for many subsequent schools for blind students.**

misfortune unlucky event
notable scholar student who stood out from the rest
prestigious highly respected
good disposition positive attitude

Memorizing was the best alternative, as students could not write, and there was little or no opportunity to access materials to read independently.

Louis was always positive and cheerful. He made good friends at the school and enjoyed activities prepared for students, such as visits to the botanical gardens in Paris. There were also music lessons, in which he continued to excel, and workshops where students like him would learn to make slippers or baskets. The condition of the school was not ideal; the building was old and cold, and there were just three teachers for 90 students of different ages and abilities, but young Louis adapted quite quickly and was soon helping his classmates.

▲ A blind boy uses his fingers to read at the Institut National des Jeunes Aveugles.

Barbier's night-writing system chart:

a	i	o	u	é	è
an	in	on	un	eu	ou
b	d	g	j	v	z
p	t	q	ch	f	s
l	m	n	r	gn	ll
oi	oin	ian	ien	ion	ieu

▲ Barbier's night-writing system

Charles Barbier de la Serre ▶

A couple of years after arriving at the school, Louis learned about a system that had been created by Charles Barbier to help soldiers in the battlefield communicate at night without making a sound. The system Barbier invented was called "night writing," and it consisted of 12 dots **embossed on paper** by means of a sharp tool. The 12 dots were arranged to represent different sounds that a person would be able to recognize by touch in the dark. The French army never adopted this system, but Barbier later thought that educators for the blind might benefit from it. Barbier took his system to the school Louis was attending.

embossed on paper raised on the page as
   bumps

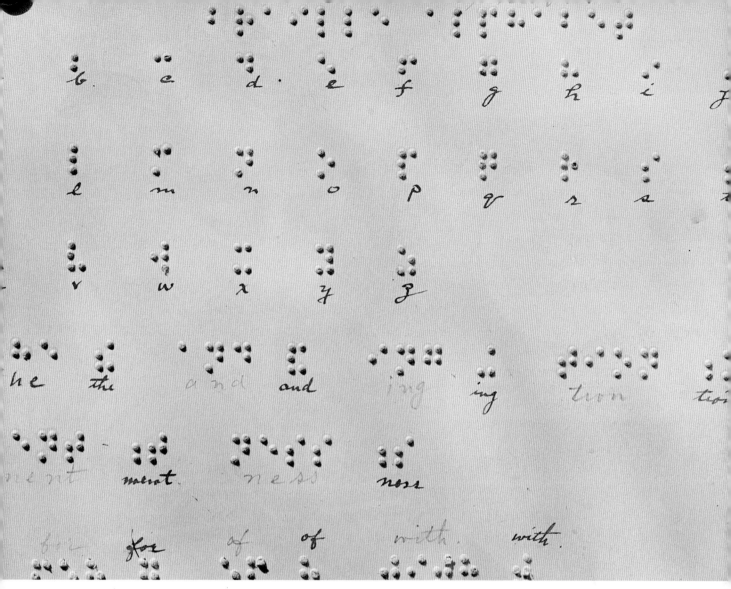

▲ **The alphabet that Louis eventually developed**

Louis was only 12 when he learned about the night-writing system, and although he saw advantages to it, he also saw disadvantages. He found the system far too complicated, which was also probably the reason French soldiers had difficulty using it on the battlefield. Not many soldiers could learn it easily. Louis thought that basing the system on sounds rather than letters was one of the factors that made it so inaccessible for people, and that 12 dots were too many. After much thought and careful analysis, Louis decided he was **capable** of simplifying this system and turning it into something easier to use.

▶ **Before You Continue**

1. **Details** Louis knew he was smart enough to simplify Barbier's code. Which details from the text support this idea?

2. **Make Inferences** How did Louis feel when he learned about Barbier's system?

▶ **Predict**
How will Louis simplify
Barbier's system?

▲ Apparatus to produce embossed
writing for blind or limited vision
people to be able to read

The French inventor
Louis Braille handling a
machine to type in braille
around 1830.

For three long years, Louis devoted much of his free time to working on his own version of Barbier's system. Instead of using 12 dots, he used six dots and arranged them in independent cells so that each one would represent a letter and not a sound. Representing letters seemed much simpler than representing the 32 French sounds. With the use of a simple **embossing tool**, the characters or cells would be **arranged** in a line so that blind people could read them by just passing their fingers over the lines.

Once the new, simpler system was created, Louis felt thrilled, as he realized how this could make life better for other **sightless** people like him. Unfortunately, his new ideas were not easily accepted by the school. Louis was just a 15-year-old kid trying to change a world where other systems were already in place. Louis's system would eliminate the need for the expensive books with raised letters that the school already had. What would happen to the people who were in charge of producing these books? Would their businesses shut down? Sighted teachers for the blind might have also felt threatened by this new system, which **implied** that blind people could teach other blind people to read and write using this new code. Regardless of whether these concerns were real, the school decided at the time not to adopt the system proposed by Louis.

This reaction did not **deter** young Louis from trying to promote his system and proving that it could work. After finishing the system for reading, he used the six-dot code for musical notation; in other words, he created a new way of reading and writing music for the blind. In 1829, he published a short and simple 32-page book with the title *Procedure for Writing Words, Music, and Plain Song in Dots,* and he became a teacher at his own school very soon afterward. As a teacher, he taught his system to his students, who adopted it quite quickly, proving that it was a better way for the blind to read and write. However, the school did not formally adopt the system at this stage, arguing that a radical change like that would be far too expensive.

embossing tool tool for pushing paper to create bumps without breaking it
arranged placed carefully
sightless blind
implied suggested
deter stop

In 1837, Louis published a three-volume history book for students using his dot system, which by then was widely known as *braille*. Braille was Louis's last name.

It would still take a few years for his school to adopt braille as the formal system of instruction, but it eventually happened. It was not only adopted by his school but, little by little, became accepted in many places beyond France, revolutionizing the educational system for the blind. Thanks to braille, blind people could easily learn and communicate with each other without the help of sighted people. Blind people started reading more and using braille to write their personal stories.

Braille became universally accepted as the code of reading and writing for the blind shortly after Louis Braille **passed away**. The system has been adapted for use in many different languages, and there are now electronic machines that simplify writing in braille for the blind. Today, technology has provided more alternatives for the blind, but braille is still a very practical solution for the **visually impaired**.

passed away died
visually impaired totally or partially blind

▲ A student from a Sri Lankan school for the blind using her braille textbook

There are many lessons to be learned from Louis Braille's life and his amazingly positive attitude. Louis was just a kid when he decided not only to learn but to transform and improve what he had learned to help blind people like him. That is what **having vision** really means. ❖

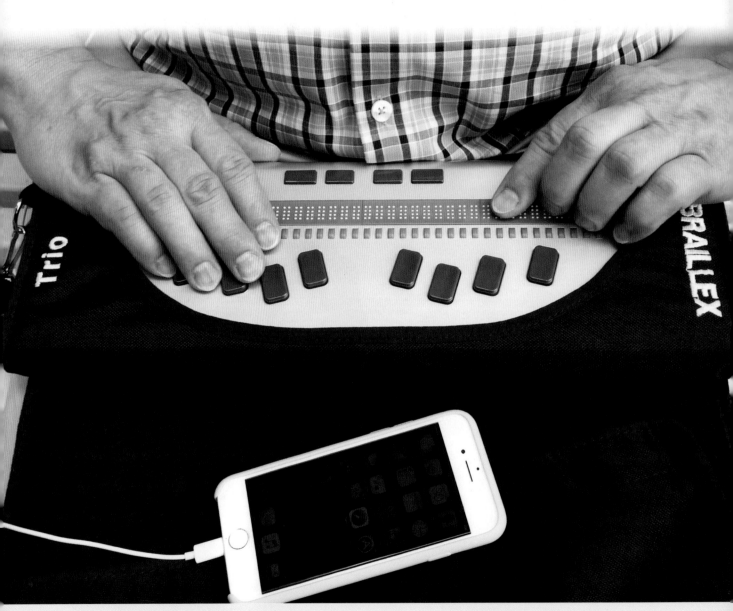

▲ A braille terminal and earphones connected to a smartphone. The terminal turns text into braille which can be perceived with the sense of touch.

having vision seeing; being thoughtful when looking toward the future

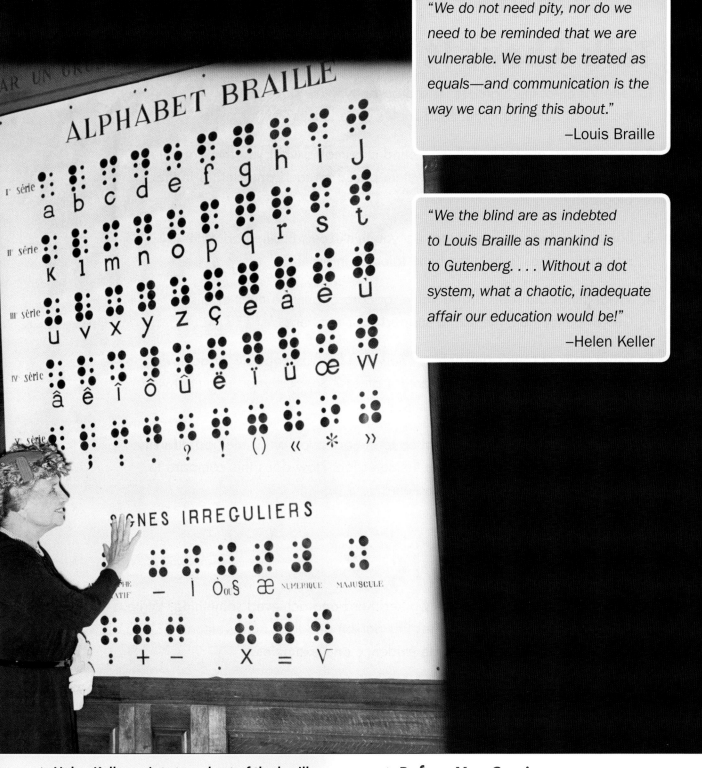

ALPHABET BRAILLE

SIGNES IRREGULIERS

"We do not need pity, nor do we need to be reminded that we are vulnerable. We must be treated as equals—and communication is the way we can bring this about."

–Louis Braille

"We the blind are as indebted to Louis Braille as mankind is to Gutenberg. . . . Without a dot system, what a chaotic, inadequate affair our education would be!"

–Helen Keller

▲ Helen Keller points to a chart of the braille alphabet during her speech at the Sorbonne, commemorating the 100th anniversary of the death of Louis Braille.

▶ **Before You Continue**

1. **Confirm Your Prediction** How did Louis Braille simplify Barbier's system? How did this affect his life?

2. **Summarize** What do we learn about Louis Braille in this text? Reread the last line of the story. How did Louis have vision?

Think and Respond

Talk About It

1. "The Vision of the Sightless" is a biography. How does the author help you understand Louis's experiences?

2. Imagine you are Louis. Tell your blind classmates what you think about Charles Barbier's night-writing system based on facts and details in the biography.

3. Based on what you have read, do you think Louis Braille had other interesting ideas to help the blind later on in his life?

4. What things did Louis Braille value, or care about, the most in this text? Cite evidence from the text to support your answer.

5. What traits of Louis's personality show that he was **capable** of achieving something important and relevant for others? Support your judgment with evidence from the text.

6. Louis Braille **encounters** **resistance** to the adoption of his method. Identify another challenge described in the selection. How does this compare to the lack of acceptance of his system?

Write About It

Think of someone you know who worked hard and achieved something. Write a biographical account that describes this person and their achievement. Include at least three **Key Words**, and include evidence and examples.

> My older sister Ikuko is very intelligent and independent, so we always made the **assumption** that she would do great things in life.

Main Idea

Use a main idea diagram to record the important details of "The Vision of the Sightless." Then use the details to determine the main idea of the selection.

Main Idea Diagram

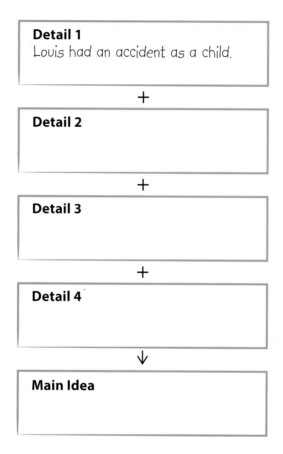

Use your main idea diagram to retell the main idea of the biography to a partner. Explain how the details helped you **figure out** the main idea.

Fluency

Practice reading with intonation. Rate your reading.

Think about the choices Louis had to make. How can difficult choices affect your life and the lives of others? Discuss your ideas with a partner. Include **Key Words** and evidence from the text.

25

Word Work

Use a Dictionary

When you read a word that has multiple meanings, try using context clues, or the nearby words and phrases, to figure out the right meaning. You may also use a print or digital **dictionary** to find all of the word's meanings and parts of speech. Then decide which meaning makes the most sense in the text you read.

EXAMPLES

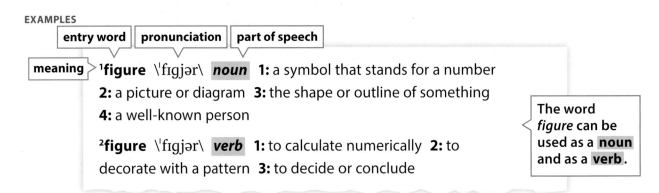

entry word | pronunciation | part of speech

meaning

¹**figure** \ˈfɪgjər\ **noun** **1:** a symbol that stands for a number **2:** a picture or diagram **3:** the shape or outline of something **4:** a well-known person

²**figure** \ˈfɪgjər\ **verb** **1:** to calculate numerically **2:** to decorate with a pattern **3:** to decide or conclude

The word *figure* can be used as a **noun** and as a **verb**.

Which definition of *figure* above best describes a famous actor or singer?

Try It

Read the sentences. Use the dictionary entries to answer the questions.

Blind people feel the bumps on the paper with their fingertips. Then they figure out what letter or symbol is being represented.

1. **Which dictionary feature helps you understand how to say figure?**

   A pronunciation

   B part of speech

   C meaning

   D example sentence

2. **Which entry gives the best meaning of figure as it is used in the sentence?**

   A ¹**figure:** definition 1

   B ¹**figure:** definition 4

   C ²**figure:** definition 2

   D ²**figure:** definition 3

A Work in **Progress**

Making Connections You read about Louis Braille's choices. Now read about how Aimee Mullins's choices changed her life.

Genre A **speech** is a message about a specific topic that is spoken before an audience.

by Aimee Mullins
as told on *The Moth Radio Hour*

Aimee Mullins has built a career as an athlete, model, actor, and **advocate for** *women, sports, and the next generation of* **prosthetics***. Mullins was born without fibular bones and had both of her legs* **amputated** *below the knee when she was an infant. She learned to walk on prosthetics, then to run— competing at national and international levels as a champion* **sprinter***, setting world records at the 1996 Paralympics in Atlanta. In 1999, Aimee made her runway debut as a model in London. She's a passionate voice heralding a new kind of thinking about bodies and identities. Aimee also has received* **accolades** *for her work as an actor on stage and film.*

advocate for *person who supports*
prosthetics *artificial body parts*
amputated *removed*
sprinter *runner*
accolades *praise; positive comments*

▶ **Before You Continue**

1. **Predict** Preview the photos and text. What do you predict the speech will be about? Read on to confirm your prediction.

2. **Draw Conclusions** What issues does Mullins care about? What makes her an effective advocate for these issues?

When I was fourteen it was Easter Sunday, and I was gonna be wearing a dress that I had purchased with my own money—the first thing I ever bought that wasn't on sale. Momentous event; you never forget it. I'd had a **paper route** since I was twelve, and I went to The Limited, and I bought this dress that I thought was the height of sophistication—sleeveless safari dress, belted, hits at the knee.

Coming downstairs into the living room, I see my father waiting to take us to church. He takes one look at me, and he says, "That doesn't look right. Go upstairs and change."

I was like, "What? My super-classy dress? What are you talking about? It's the best thing I own."

He said, "No, you can see the knee joint when you walk. It doesn't look right. It's inappropriate to go out like that. Go change."

And I think something snapped in me. I refused to change. And it was the first time I **defied** my father. I refused to hide something about myself that was true, and I refused to be embarrassed about something so that other people could feel more comfortable.

I was **grounded** for that defiance.

So after church the extended family convenes at my grandmother's house and everybody's complimenting me on how nice I look in this dress and I'm like, "Really? You think I look nice? Because my parents think I look inappropriate."

I **outed them** (kinda mean, really).

But I think **the public utterance of** this idea that I should somehow hide myself was so shocking to hear that it changed their mind about why they were doing it.

And I had always managed to get through life with somewhat of a positive attitude, but I think this was the start of me being able to accept myself. You know, okay, I'm not normal. I have strengths. I've got weaknesses. It is what it is.

And I had always been athletic, but it wasn't until college that I started this adventure in Track and Field. I had gone through a lifetime of being given legs that just barely got me by. And I thought, Well, maybe I'm just having the wrong conversations with the wrong people. Maybe I need to go find people who say, "Yes, we can create anything for you in the space between where your leg ends and the ground."

paper route job delivering newspapers
defied disobeyed
grounded punished
outed them told everyone what they had done
the public utterance saying

▶ **Before You Continue**

1. **Confirm Prediction** What is the main focus of Mullins's speech so far? Revise your prediction or form a new one.

2. **Explain** Why was Mullins's decision about the dress an important event for her and her parents? How did they each respond?

And so I started working with engineers, fashion designers, sculptors, Hollywood prosthetic makeup artists, and wax museum designers to build legs for me.

I decided I wanted to be the fastest woman in the world on prosthetic legs and I was lucky enough to **arrive in track** at just the right time to be the first person to get these radical sprinting legs modeled after the hind leg of a cheetah, the fastest thing that runs—woven carbon fiber. I was able to set three world records with those legs. And they made no attempt at **approximating humanness**.

Then I get these incredibly lifelike silicon legs—hand-painted, capillaries, veins. And, hey, I can be as tall as I wanna be, so I get different legs for different heights. I don't have to shave. I can wear open-toed shoes in the winter. And most importantly, I can **opt out of the cankles** I most certainly would've inherited genetically.

And then I get these legs made for me by **the late, great Alexander McQueen**, and they were hand-carved of solid ash with grapevines and magnolias all over them and a six-inch heel. And I was able to walk the runways of the world with supermodels. I was suddenly in this whirlwind of adventure and excitement. I was being invited to go around the world and speak about these adventures, and how I had legs that looked like glass, legs covered in feathers, porcelain legs, jellyfish legs—all wearable sculpture.

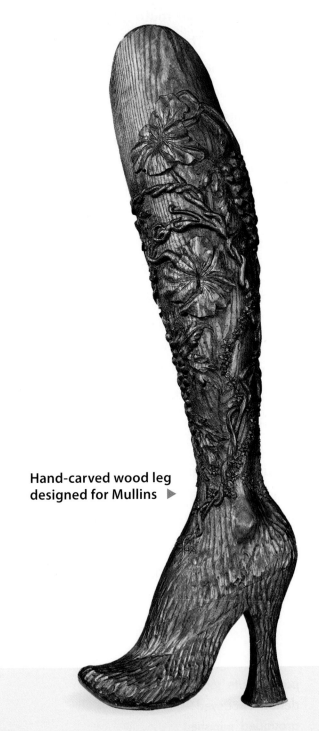

Hand-carved wood leg designed for Mullins ▶

arrive in track start competing in Track and Field
approximating humanness pretending to look like normal legs
opt out of the cankles avoid getting the unattractive ankles
the late, great Alexander McQueen a famous clothing designer

Mullins competing in the women's long jump event at the Paralympics

▶ **Before You Continue**

1. **Cause/Effect** How did Mullins's new legs affect her life? Cite evidence from the speech to support your response.

2. **Author's Viewpoint** What is Mullins's opinion about having legs made from unusual materials?

A prosthetic limb doesn't represent the need to replace loss anymore. It can stand as a symbol that the wearer has the power to create whatever it is they want to create.

—Aimee Mullins

And I get this call from a guy who had seen me speak years ago, when I was at the beginning of my track career, and he says, "We loved it. We want you to come back." And it was clear to me he didn't know all these amazing things that had happened to me since my sports career.

So as I'm telling him, he says, "Whoa, whoa, whoa. Hold on, Aimee. The reason everybody liked you all those years ago was because you were this sweet, **vulnerable**, **naïve** girl, and if you walk onstage today, and you are this **polished** young woman with too many accomplishments, I'm afraid they won't like you."

For real, he said that. Wow.

He apparently didn't think I was vulnerable enough now. He was asking me to be less than, a little more **downtrodden**. He was asking me to disable myself for him and his audience.

And what was so shocking to me about that was that I realized I had moved past mere acceptance of my difference. I was having fun with my difference. Thank God I'm not normal. I get to be extraordinary. And I'll decide what is a weakness and what is a strength.

And so I refused his request.

vulnerable helpless
naïve innocent
polished confident and successful
downtrodden hopeless and needy

And a few days later, I'm walking in downtown Manhattan at a street fair, and I get this tug on my shirt, and I look down. It's this little girl I met a year earlier when she was at a **pivotal** moment in her life. She had been born with a brittle bone disease that resulted in her left leg being seven centimeters shorter than her right. She wore **a brace and orthopedic shoes** and they **got her by**, but she wanted to do more.

And like all **Internet-savvy** kindergarteners, she gets on the computer and Googles "new leg," and she comes up with dozens of images of prosthetics, many of them mine.

And she prints them out, goes to school, **does show-and-tell on it**, comes home, and makes a startling pronouncement to her parents: "I wanna get rid of my bad leg," she says. "When can I get a new leg?"

And ultimately that was the decision her parents and doctors made for her. So here she was, six months after the amputation, and right there in the middle of the street fair, she hikes up her jeans leg to show me her cool new leg. And it's pink, and it's tattooed with the characters of *High School Musical 3*, replete with red, sequined Mary Janes on her feet.

And she was proud of it. She was proud of herself. And the marvelous thing was that this six-year-old understood something that took me twenty-something years to get, but that we both did discover—that when we can celebrate and truly own what it is that makes us different, we're able to find the source of our greatest creative power.

Thank you. ❖

pivotal very important
a brace and orthopedic shoes equipment on her legs
got her by helped her walk
Internet-savvy computer-using
does a show-and-tell on it tells her class about it

▸ **Before You Continue**

1. **Author's Viewpoint** How does Mullins feel about being "different"? What details support your answer?

2. **Make Inferences** What advice would Mullins give to someone who is facing challenges in life?

Compare Main Ideas

"The Vision of the Sightless" and "A Work in Progress" both include choices. Use a comparison chart to compare the main ideas and important details from these texts. Then synthesize, or put together, the ideas in the chart to tell what they show about Louis Braille and Aimee Mullins.

Comparison Chart

	"The Vision of the Sightless"	"A Work in Progress"
genre	biography	
main idea		
author's choice		

Talk Together

How do the two selections help you understand the ways that choices can affect people's lives? Use text evidence and **Key Words** to talk about your ideas with a small group.

Complete Sentences

A sentence expresses a complete thought. A **complete sentence** has two parts: a subject and a predicate. The **subject** is who or what the sentence is about. The **predicate** is what the subject is, does, or has.

Grammar Rules Complete Sentences

The **complete subject** includes all the words that tell about the subject. The **simple subject** is the most important noun or nouns in the subject.	**A bright, young girl** spoke to Aimee Mullins.
The **complete predicate** includes the verb and all the other words in the predicate. The **simple predicate** is the main verb in the predicate.	A bright, young girl **spoke** to **Aimee Mullins**

Read Complete Sentences

Writers and speakers use complete subjects and predicates to expand their ideas and provide more details about the subject and verb. Read this passage based on "A Work in Progress." Find the complete and simple subject and the complete and simple predicate in each sentence.

> Model and athlete Aimee Mullins speaks about her prosthetic legs. The large audience listens to her story. Her prosthetic legs fascinate them. Mullins's amazing courage is inspiring as well.

Write Complete Sentences

Reread page 33. Write three complete sentences to explain how you would change the way people think about disabilities. Then trade sentences with a partner, and find the complete and simple subjects and the complete and simple predicates in each other's sentences.

Language Focus

Ask and Answer Questions

Listen to the interview. Then use the **Language Frames** to interview a partner. Ask and answer questions about each other, making sure to elaborate and give details in your responses.

Who Are You?

Eva: Dana, I noticed you always write something in that notebook, even at break time. Why do you write all the time?

Dana: This is my personal notepad. I write observations of everything I see, and I also write what I think. Writing is my hobby.

Eva: Can you explain more about your hobby?

Dana: Sure! I write things I observe and then my feelings and opinions. When I reread what I've written, if I notice I have a good idea or something, I write a better version, and I publish it in a blog. Writing in my blog is really important to me.

Eva: Wow! That's interesting. Why do you have a blog?

Dana: Well, when I share ideas and thoughts with other people, I can get comments and feedback. That helps me learn from others and also makes me think about the way I write. If I'm not clear enough, others can get confused with what I'm trying to say. I like sharing ideas with people and hearing from them.

Social Studies Vocabulary

Key Words

Key Words
associate
confront
preservation
sensitive
tolerance

◀) Key Words

Look at the photographs and read the opinion. Use **Key Words** and
other words to talk about the choices people make about their hobbies or interests.

Our world is filled with people with many differences in taste and personality.
Because we are not all the same, it is important to be aware of and **sensitive** to
people's interests and ideas. We should never judge or **confront** people who choose
to do something we wouldn't choose for ourselves. Instead, we should treat people
with respect, acceptance, and **tolerance** because this is a world where we all can
learn from each other.

Many people decide their interests or make choices about their hobbies because
they are influenced by close friends or family members, who are looking for
the **preservation** of what they consider a tradition. This is not a bad idea, but we
should also **associate** with people with different interests, so that we can learn about
new activities that might suit our talents or personalities better.

Talk **Together**

What choices do people make about their hobbies and interests? What choices do you
make to understand the interests of others? Use **Language Frames** from page 36 and
Key Words to pose and respond to questions with a partner. Remember to elaborate
on your ideas and include comments that contribute to your discussion of the topic.

37

Characters and Plot

In fiction, the **characters** are the people that the story is about. The **plot** is the series of episodes, or events, that make up the story. In many stories, the way that characters respond to events may change and influence what happens next.

In the following passage, a girl named Mia makes a choice that becomes an important plot event in the story. Look for ways that Mrs. Mendoza responds and changes because of this event.

Look Into the Text

"**I can't publish this**."

Mrs. Mendoza looked up. "Why not?"

"It's not the truth," I said. "It causes harm. The cafeteria is helping students, not hurting them. This isn't responsible journalism."

Mrs. Mendoza frowned. "Can you edit the story so it's true?"

I nodded and quickly pounded out a revised—truthful—article.

Mrs. Mendoza read it. "Let's publish."

After learning about Mia's **choice**, Mrs. Mendoza **responds**. She reads Mia's new story and changes what she was going to do.

Map and Talk

You can use a character-and-plot chart to record information about how characters respond and change as the plot moves from the beginning to the end of the story.

Character-and-Plot Chart

Character	Plot Event	Response
Mrs. Mendoza	reads Mia's edited story	

Talk Together

Tell a partner about a time that someone you know made an important decision. How did you respond? What did you do? Your partner completes a character-and-plot chart and uses it to retell your story.

🔊 More Key Words

Use these words to talk about "Hot off the Press" and "The Spark of Determination."

awareness
noun

When you have **awareness** of something, you see or understand it. They used their **awareness** of traffic and safety rules to cross the street.

conform
verb

When you **conform**, you follow a rule or way of doing things. In some schools, all students must **conform** to a dress code by wearing a uniform.

intent
noun

An **intent** is a plan to do something. The student studies hard with the **intent** of passing a difficult test.

interaction
noun

An **interaction** is when people talk or do activities with one another. This is an **interaction** between three friends.

involve
verb

To **involve** means to include. Winning a baseball game may **involve** speed, strength, and teamwork.

Talk Together

Make a Word Map for each **Key Word**. Then compare your maps with a partner's.

Definition: follow a rule	Characteristics: being like others
Example: go to school on time	Non-example: go to school late

conform

Learn to Monitor

As you read, make sure you understand the text. If there is something you do not understand, you can stop to **monitor**, or check, your progress.

How to Monitor

?	**1.** When you do not understand part of the text, stop reading. Think about what the text means.	I'm confused about _____.
👁	**2.** If you still do not understand, reread the text or read on. Use context clues or vocabulary resources to understand unknown words. If the text is still unclear, ask for help.	I _____ to help me _____.
☁	**3.** Think about how doing these things helps you better understand the text.	Now I understand _____.

Here's how one student monitored her reading.

Look Into the Text

The class started talking about how to save the *Beacon*.

"We need a **blockbuster** story," said Olivia. "Something to involve students. **Something everybody reads. Something everybody talks about.**"

The staff brainstormed story ideas.

"I'm confused about the **word** *blockbuster*. I find **evidence** to help me see what the students are trying to achieve. Now I understand that *blockbuster* means 'really big and successful.'"

As you read, pause to monitor your understanding of the text. Try to clarify each misunderstanding as you encounter it.

Read the interview and sample notes. Use **Language Frames** to monitor as you read. Then talk with a partner about how you monitored your reading.

Language Frames

I'm confused about _____ .

I _____ to help me _____ .

Now I understand _____ .

Interview

A NEW HOBBY FOR HAN

Andrew: Last year you told me your sister was a vlogger. Do you remember that?

Han: [*laughing*] I remember that! I remember you thought I was mispronouncing the word. I had to spell it for you, and then you thought I was making a mistake. You thought I meant blogger.

Andrew: That was funny! But I'm still not sure there is a real difference between a blogger and a vlogger. Can you remind me again? ◄

Han: Well, the use of video is the main difference. A blogger is someone who writes their personal opinions or experiences and then publishes them online. A vlog **involves** the use of video to tell others about their experiences. Vloggers don't write; they speak to people.

Andrew: This is where I get confused, because I see writing, video, audio, and photos from both bloggers and vloggers. And the **intent** is the same in both: to share personal ideas and experiences, right? I also see that both invite **interaction** with others. ◄

Han: You're right about the intent and the interaction! But they're easy to differentiate if you just consider the main media they use. Bloggers expect you to read. They may use other media to include information **associated** with what they wrote, but this material is supplementary. Vloggers expect you to watch their video, mainly. ◄

Andrew: Oh, I see now. Does your sister still vlog?

Han: Yes, she does! And she's teaching me how to do it. In my country, you cannot vlog until you're 16 or older, but she thinks I need to be ready if I want to do it in the future.

Andrew: Do you think you'll want to do it? Sometimes when you publish your ideas online, you're **confronted** by others who think differently.

Han: Yes, I know. But you have to be prepared not to be too **sensitive** and also to be open to listening to others. If you want to raise **awareness** on a certain topic, or even just discuss your points of view with others, you have to understand that we're all different so **tolerance**, respect, and openness are important for the **preservation** of true communication. Wouldn't you agree?

I'm confused about the difference between a *blog* and a *vlog*.

I read on to help me find an answer.

Now I understand that *blogs* are mostly words, *vlogs* are mostly video.

◄ = a good place to stop and monitor your reading

Read Realistic Fiction

Genre

A **realistic fiction** story tells about events that could happen in real life. It includes realistic characters, settings, and plot events.

Narrator

In fiction, the **narrator** is the person who tells the story. The narrator can be a character who is describing the events or someone who isn't directly involved in the story. In "Hot off the Press," the narrator is a female character named Mia. She uses words like *I*, *me*, and *my* to tell the story.

> **I** quietly opened **my** notebook. **I** was afraid if **I** made a noise, she would notice **me** and realize she'd made a mistake.

HOT OFF THE PRESS

by Lisa Harkrader

▶ Set a Purpose
Find out what happens when Mia
makes an important choice.

Journalistic Code of Ethics
1. Seek truth and report it.
2. Minimize harm.
3. Act independently.
4. Be accountable and transparent.

I slipped into Mrs. Mendoza's room and found a seat in the back. I watched the other kids **trickle in**. They'd been on the newspaper a while, and they were older—a bunch of older kids, plus me.

My heart **thundered**. I couldn't believe Mrs. Mendoza had actually let me in, let me **associate** with her seasoned reporters. I quietly opened my notebook. I was afraid if I made a noise, she would notice me and realize she'd made a mistake.

But she didn't.

Instead, she smiled and said, "Mia! Welcome to the newspaper staff."

"The Prairie School *Beacon* has a tradition of **high standards**," Mrs. Mendoza told the class. "We **conform** to a journalistic **code of ethics**."

Journalistic code of ethics! I blinked. This was better than I'd even hoped.

"We **seek** truth and report it," said Mrs. Mendoza.

I nodded. I'd been seeking truth and reporting it on my own blog. My **intent** was to gain journalistic experience, but when I showed it to Mrs. Mendoza, she invited me to be on the newspaper.

I smiled. She probably saw that I already had an **awareness** of journalistic ethics.

trickle in enter gradually
thundered beat loudly
high standards expecting the best
code of ethics set of rules about what is right and wrong
seek look for

Mrs. Mendoza talked more about ethics. "In our reporting, we **minimize harm**. We act independently. And we keep ourselves accountable and **transparent**. That means we take responsibility for our work."

Then she gave us our assignments.

She appointed Olivia as editor and Marcus as assistant editor. That made sense. They'd both been on the paper a long time. She named the reporters and photojournalists. I held my breath, waiting for my name. She assigned the copy editors and advertising staff. I swallowed. She'd forgotten me.

"And last but not least," she said, "Mia, our website assistant."

Website assistant?

My heart **slumped**. I knew I had to start somewhere. I couldn't be editor-in-chief on my first day.

But...website assistant?

"We're lucky to have Mia," Mrs. Mendoza told the class. "She publishes her own **blog**, and it looks amazing. We need someone with her skills to put the *Beacon* online."

"It has to look **dynamic**," said Marcus.

"It has to *be* dynamic," said Olivia. "Now more than ever."

"Why now more than ever?" I said.

"If we can't get more students reading it," Mrs. Mendoza explained, "the school may shut the *Beacon* down."

minimize harm try not to do things that hurt people
transparent honest; not secretive
slumped moved downward heavily; sagged
blog online journal
dynamic full of energy; exciting

The class started talking about how to save the *Beacon*.

"We need a blockbuster story," said Olivia. "Something to **involve** students. Something everybody reads. Something everybody talks about."

The staff **brainstormed** story ideas.

I worked up my courage. "I could write something," I said.

Olivia frowned. "We need someone to **cover** the lunchroom. The lunch menu and stuff."

Lunch. Tears burned my throat, but I nodded. If I was the lunch reporter, I was going to do the best lunch reporting the *Beacon* had ever seen.

I snatched my notebook and headed to the cafeteria.

brainstormed worked together to figure out
cover report about

Olivia had said to cover the menu *and* **stuff**. I glanced around the lunchroom, looking for stuff.

Kids crowded through the line, getting food, clattering silverware. No good stuff there.

Then I saw a boy named Andre. He slipped through a door behind the cashier—a door only cafeteria workers used.

I raised an eyebrow. *This* could be interesting. I followed him.

The door led to a small room. Andre and other kids were lined up at a counter. Mrs. Jackson, the cafeteria supervisor, handed them trays.

I blinked. I'd uncovered a secret lunch line!

stuff other nonspecific things

▶ **Before You Continue**

1. **Clarify** Why is a code of ethics important for a newspaper?
2. **Make Inferences** How does Mia feel about the assignments she is given? Cite evidence from the text.

Mrs. Jackson frowned. "Mia? Do you have **food allergies**?"

"Uh, no," I said. "I'm from the *Beacon*."

She smiled. "Writing a story about the special diet line."

"Special diet?" I asked.

Mrs. Jackson nodded. "For kids who are **sensitive** to certain foods."

She explained that the school had started providing a separate line for
students who didn't have a **tolerance** for foods like milk, nuts, or wheat.

"Food allergies can be dangerous," she said.

Andre laughed. "Mrs. Jackson doesn't want to
accidentally poison me with a peanut."

I took pages of notes about the special diet line.

food allergies a medical condition where certain
   foods make you sick

accidentally poison me with a peanut give me a
   food that makes me sick without meaning to

By the time I got back to Mrs. Mendoza's room, I'd **practically** written the article in my head. I **pitched my story idea** to Olivia and Marcus.

Olivia chewed her lip. "This may be exactly what we need."

Marcus nodded. "It could get students reading and talking. Everyone has some kind of **interaction** with the lunchroom."

"**With the right angle**, it could be a blockbuster," said Olivia. "Thanks for the **tip**, Mia. I'll write this for our first edition."

I blinked. "But I—"

She marched off to her computer, my notes in her hand.

practically almost

pitched my story idea told what I wanted to write about

With the right angle If we present it in a certain way

tip idea; suggestion

The *Beacon* staff spent the week writing articles and taking photos. I typed up the lunch menu.

Finally it was time for the website assistant—me—to put everything online. Olivia sent me her article. I stared at the headline: CAFETERIA **NEARLY** POISONS STUDENT.

Olivia smiled. "Our blockbuster."

I never liked to **confront** anybody. But the journalistic code of ethics **meant something**.

I swallowed. "I can't publish this."

Mrs. Mendoza looked up. "Why not?"

"It's not the truth," I said. "It causes harm. The cafeteria is helping students, not hurting them. This isn't responsible journalism."

NEARLY ALMOST
meant something was important

Mrs. Mendoza frowned. "Can you **edit** the story so it's true?"

I nodded and quickly **pounded out** a revised—truthful—article.

Mrs. Mendoza read it. "Let's publish."

"Fine," said Olivia. "But when nobody reads it, it won't be *my* fault."

But everyone *did* read it. And talked about it. And left comments online.

On Monday, Mrs. Mendoza had an announcement. "The school administration loved our reporting. They want us to continue."

The class cheered.

Mrs. Mendoza smiled at me. "You may turn into a journalist yet. You're the best reporter **on the lunchroom beat**." ❖

edit change; rewrite
pounded out worked fast to create
on the lunchroom beat who reports on events of the cafeteria

▶ **Before You Continue**

1. **Make Comparisons** How is Mia's choice different from Olivia's?
2. **Point of View** How does Mia's point of view as narrator affect the story? Cite examples from the text.

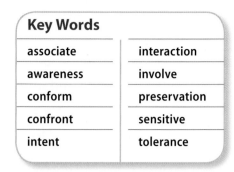

Key Words

associate	interaction
awareness	involve
conform	preservation
confront	sensitive
intent	tolerance

Talk About It

1. "Hot off the Press" is realistic fiction. What are some details in Mia's story that remind you of real **interactions** between people in your school?

2. Compare Mia and Olivia's viewpoints, or opinions, about Mia's choice to publish an honest article. Use evidence from the text to support the comparison.

3. What questions do you still have about Mia, her experiences, or her article at the end of the story? Look back into the text to ask and answer questions you are still thinking about.

4. Using examples from the text, analyze how Mia's sense of responsibility helps her **confront** tough situations.

5. Many people feel that they need to **conform** to the rules and ideas of people around them. How do you think Mia would respond to this attitude? Explain your opinion using evidence from the text.

6. What is an important theme, or message, of the story? How do the characters and plot events support this theme?

Write About It

Write an email from Mia to a friend at her school to explain her decision. Use at least three **Key Words** and support your ideas with evidence from the text.

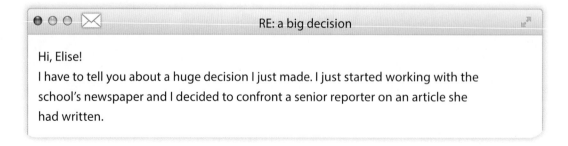

● ● ● ✉ RE: a big decision

Hi, Elise!
I have to tell you about a huge decision I just made. I just started working with the school's newspaper and I decided to confront a senior reporter on an article she had written.

Characters and Plot

Use a character-and-plot chart to record how different characters respond to the events in "Hot off the Press."

Character-and-Plot Chart

Character	Plot Event	Response
Mrs. Mendoza	asks Mia to rewrite the article	

Use your character-and-plot chart to retell the story to a partner. Describe Mia's choice and how characters respond and change in response to the plot events. Use **Key Words**.

Fluency

Practice reading with expression. Rate your reading.

Mia's choices affect her success. What are some ways that choices affect your life? Discuss your ideas with a partner. Use **Key Words**.

Word Work

Use a Thesaurus

A **thesaurus** is a reference that lists synonyms and antonyms. Synonyms are words with similar meanings, like *intent* and *plan.* Antonyms are words with opposite meanings, like *conform* and *rebel.* When you write, you can use a thesaurus to find the best words to express your ideas.

EXAMPLES

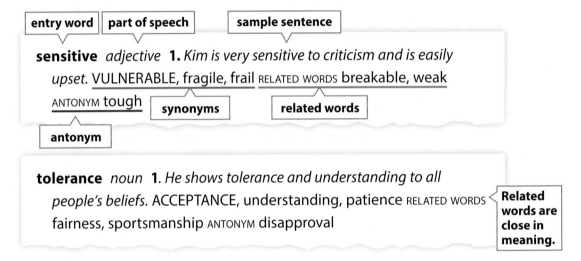

| entry word | part of speech | | sample sentence |

sensitive *adjective* **1.** *Kim is very sensitive to criticism and is easily upset.* VULNERABLE, fragile, frail RELATED WORDS breakable, weak ANTONYM tough

synonyms   related words   antonym

tolerance *noun* **1.** *He shows tolerance and understanding to all people's beliefs.* ACCEPTANCE, understanding, patience RELATED WORDS fairness, sportsmanship ANTONYM disapproval

> **Related words are close in meaning.**

Try It

Read the sentences. Then use the thesaurus entries above to answer the questions.

> Mia was <u>sensitive</u> about being a new student on the newspaper staff.
> Mrs. Mendoza showed <u>tolerance</u> and listened to Mia's ideas.

1. You want to replace the word <u>sensitive</u>. Which word is the best synonym to replace it?

   A breakable

   B tough

   C frail

   D vulnerable

2. You want to replace the word <u>tolerance</u>. Which is the best synonym to replace it?

   A patience

   B fairness

   C disapproval

   D sportsmanship

THE SPARK
of DETERMINATION

by Laura A. Meza

Sparky got his nickname from the "Barney Google" comic.

There are times in our lives when one decision affects the rest of what is to come, but more often than not, it is the brave, **unwavering** choices that guide who we are and help us find our true talents and successes. This is what happened in the story of Sparky, a boy who chose to **pursue his dreams** instead of taking the easy path in life.

A few years after his birth on November 26, 1922, Charles, the only child of a Minnesota couple, was given the nickname of "Sparky" by an uncle, who got the idea from a comic strip that was popular back then. Family members adopted this nickname, and it remained with him for the rest of his life.

unwavering firm; decisive
pursue his dreams work toward what
   he wanted most

▶ **Before You Continue**
1. **Point of View** Who is telling Sparky's story? Which specific words and ideas in the text indicate this point of view?
2. **Predict** Based on what you have read, what do you think Sparky's choice will be related to?

Sparky's parents were not highly educated, but they were good, hardworking people. Sparky's father was very young when he decided to get work **pitching hay** in Nebraska so he could pay for a course to become a barber. Years later, he opened his own **barbershop**, and this made his son proud. This is probably how young Sparky learned to work hard, learn a trade, and persist toward his goals.

Growing up, a lot of his time was spent at his dad's barbershop. On Sunday mornings, Sparky always read the **funnies** with his dad. Comic strips were loved by both father and son, and they always bought more than one local newspaper so they would have access to the various strips they enjoyed reading, such as *Skippy, Buck Rogers, Mickey Mouse,* and *Popeye*. At school, Sparky realized he enjoyed drawing, and he **was particularly flattered and motivated** when a teacher told him he could become an artist. He became interested in learning how to draw better.

pitching hay in the fields on a farm
barbershop business giving haircuts and shaves
funnies comic strip section in the newspaper
was particularly flattered and motivated felt good and wanted to try harder

As an elementary school student, he developed a passion for ice hockey, a sport he would continue to love forever. He also had a lot of love for the family dogs. They had a black Boston Bull Terrier named Spooky, and then, after she passed away, a black and white mixed-breed dog named Spike, which was intelligent and fun to be around. But Sparky's true love was comic strips, and he grew up dreaming of one day being able to draw his own comics.

Inspired by that dream, Sparky, at age 14, drew the family dog, Spike, and he and his dad sent the picture to a magazine. They wrote about how Spike would eat all sorts of strange things, such as pins and razor blades. The magazine published the drawing, giving Sparky his first taste of success as a cartoonist.

In spite of this first small but happy achievement, Sparky's teenage years were not easy. He was shy and kept to himself a lot. Others perceived him as a good kid but also an anxious one. In his senior year, he decided to submit cartoons to his high school yearbook, but the student committee in charge did not publish them. Despite this disappointment, Sparky did not give up. He kept drawing. Drawing and cartoons remained his main hobby and ambition. It was time to think about his future. Could he turn this into a career?

▲ Cartoonist/ illustrator Charles M. Schulz with one of his family's five dogs in California

▶ **Before You Continue**

1. **Plot** What is the choice Sparky has to make? Confirm or change your prediction.

2. **Make Inferences** What struggles did Sparky have as a teenager? Why were his drawings rejected at school?

At 18 years old, Sparky decided to take a course in drawing. He graduated from high school and started doing different jobs, but he could not stop thinking about the world of cartoons and illustrations. He sent his drawings and ideas to different magazines, always getting rejection letters. He also applied to work as an animator for Walt Disney, but he was turned down from that, too. He then **enlisted** in the army.

After serving as a sergeant for the United States Army in World War II, Sparky came home determined to do what he loved. He was finally offered a job that was more in line with his artistic inclinations. He became an art instructor for Art Instruction Schools, Inc.—the same school where he had previously taken his drawing course. Things were looking up, but making his own comic was still his dream.

He did not give up. He kept writing and trying to sell his cartoons. He drew about things he knew until finally, he sold a strip called **Li'l Folks** by Sparky. This strip was about a young boy like the one he had been: shy and with little success, owner of a black and white dog he loved. Charlie Brown and Snoopy came to life in this way. The strip was well received and would evolve to become *Peanuts*, an **endearing**

comic series that Sparky, better known as Charles Schulz, would draw for the rest of his life.

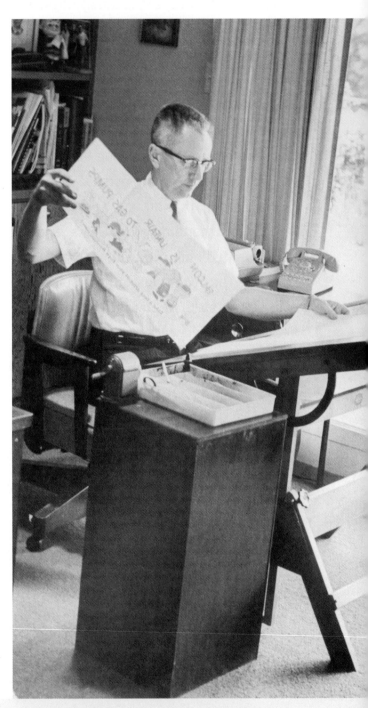

▲ **Charles Schulz worked on the same drawing board he purchased at the beginning of his career.**

enlisted signed up
Li'l Folks small children
endearing sweet; loveable

The name Charles Schulz is now known all over the world. His characters Charlie Brown, Linus, Lucy, Snoopy, and Woodstock are among the most loved and recognized cartoon images ever created. Charlie Brown, the boy who never seems to win, and Snoopy, the clever black and white dog born from the inspiration of Sparky's real-life dog Spike, are at the center of Schulz's creations. In his comics, these characters are surrounded by other children who seem to feel and talk like small adults but who are funny and sweet at the same time. Part of the success of *Peanuts* is the intelligent and special kind of humor his characters convey, all presented within a reality most of us can identify with and in a style of drawing that was **innovative** in its day.

Sparky's dream came true, and he achieved even more. By not letting failure cloud the love he had for drawing, and by deciding to **persevere toward** his goal, he not only gave people a comic strip to keep themselves entertained; he also lived to be an example we can all learn from. ❖

The characters Schulz created are now known around the world, shown in comics, TV shows, and movies.

innovative new and different
persevere toward work hard to achieve

▶ **Before You Continue**
1. **Plot** What was Sparky's unwavering decision? How did he finally succeed?
2. **Make Inferences** What was Sparky's attitude toward failure? Cite evidence from the text to support your ideas.

Key Words	
associate	interaction
awareness	involve
conform	preservation
confront	sensitive
intent	tolerance

Compare Characters

"Hot off the Press" and "The Spark of Determination" both **involve** choices that people make. Use a chart to compare the characters' responses to their problems. Then analyze the information and explain what it shows about the two characters.

Narrator/Character Chart

	"Hot off the Press"	"The Spark of Determination"
Narrator or Main Character	Mia	Sparky
Problem		
Thoughts and Feelings		
Choices		
Actions and Responses		

Talk Together

How do both of the selections show ways that choices can affect the way people respond to you? Use **Key Words** and text evidence to discuss your ideas with a small group.

Subject-Verb Agreement

The subject and verb of a sentence must agree in number.

Grammar Rules Subject-Verb Agreement	
The verb you use depends on the noun in the subject. Choose the right **verb** for singular or plural **subjects**.	**Mia wants** to be a reporter. **Journalists conform** to a code of ethics.
If the **nouns** in a **compound subject** are connected by **and**, use a **verb** that goes with plural nouns.	**Mia and Olivia disagree** on the article about the cafeteria.
If the nouns in a **compound subject** are connected by **or** or **nor**, look at the **last noun**. Determine whether the noun is singular or plural. Use the **verb** that matches the noun.	Either **the classmates or the teacher explains** the problem. Neither **the teacher nor the students support** Mia in the beginning.

Read Sentences with Correct Subject-Verb Agreement

To keep their writing clear, good writers make sure their subjects and verbs agree. Read this passage based on "Hot off the Press." Identify the subject and verb in each sentence. Explain how you know why the subjects and verbs agree.

> Mrs. Mendoza introduces Mia to the journalism class. Mrs. Mendoza and two students explain the newspaper needs to be dynamic. Mia asks why.

Write Sentences with Correct Subject-Verb Agreement

Reread pages 52–53 of "Hot off the Press." Write a short paragraph that describes the problem that Mia and Olivia have about the article. Include one sentence with a singular subject, one with a plural subject, and one with a compound subject. Make sure each verb agrees with its subject. Then compare your sentences with a partner's.

Write About Yourself

Write a Personal Narrative ✎

Write about a time when you had to make a choice. Then add your story to a class book about choices.

Study a Model

A personal narrative is a true story about something that happened to you. You are the narrator telling about the events. Read Li's story about a choice she made.

The Audition
by Li Stewart

The beginning introduces the problem.

When I grow up, I want to be a choreographer. Nothing would be more fun than making up dances for a living! When the dance studio announced auditions for a student-choreographed dance show, I felt both excited and scared. How could I get the job?

Li tells how she responded to the events.

She organizes the events in sequence and uses transitions to make the sequence clear.

With the auditions only a month away, I had to choose music and create my dance steps. First, I picked my favorite song. Next, I tried out dance moves. For the soft, trilling part of the music, I waved my arms like a bird. For the loud, rhythmic part, I moved with sharp, jagged steps. Then, I looked at dance videos for more ideas. At last, I was ready!

She uses vivid language to help readers picture the events.

The ending tells whether Li's problem is solved.

Two weeks later, I stepped onto the stage. The first part went fine, but then I missed a jump. I was so upset that I wanted to give up right there. But then I made a choice: I would do my best and never give up! I took a deep breath and let the music and all my rehearsing take over. After the last chord, I bowed to the judges and smiled to myself. I had done it!

Prewrite

1. **Choose a Topic** What experience will you write about? Talk with a partner to choose a time in your life when you had to make a choice.

Language Frames	
Tell Your Ideas	**Respond to Ideas**
• An important choice I made recently was _____ .	• Why was _____ an important choice for you?
• I remember when I _____ .	• How did you _____ ?
• One thing that happened to me was _____ .	• What happened when _____ ?

Use sentences and questions like these to help you decide about a topic.

2. **Gather Information** Collect precise words and descriptive details that tell about your experience and the order of events. Write your feelings, and tell what happened because of your choice.

3. **Get Organized** Use a sequence chain to help organize your ideas.

Sequence Chain

Beginning
I had to prepare a dance for an audition.

↓

Middle
• I made up dance moves for my music.
• I looked at dance videos and got more ideas.

↓

End
• I was proud that I didn't give up and finished the audition.

Draft

Use your sequence chain and the details you collected to write your draft. Tell what happened and how you responded to the events. Give descriptive details to develop the experience. Use transition words as you describe the events.

Revise

1. **Read, Retell, Respond** Read your draft aloud to a partner. Your partner listens and then retells the story. Then talk about ways to improve your writing.

Language Frames	
Retell	**Make Suggestions**
• The choice you made was _____ .	• The sequence of events isn't clear. Could you add a transition, such as _____ ?
• In the beginning, you _____ . After that, you _____ . At the end, you _____ .	• I really like the part about _____ . Can you add more descriptive details to help me picture it?
• The details you included are _____ .	• I'm not sure how you felt about _____ . Maybe you could include _____ .
• You felt _____ about _____ .	

Use sentences like these to respond to your partner's writing.

2. **Make Changes** Think about your draft and your partner's suggestions. Use revision marks to make your changes.

   • Make sure you have sequenced story events logically and used transition words to make the sequence clear.

   > Next,
   > I tried out dance moves.
   > First,
   > I chose my favorite song.

   • Do you have enough descriptive details? Would adding details help convey events more clearly?

   > the soft, trilling   like a bird
   > For part of the music, I waved my arms.

Edit and Proofread

Work with a partner to edit and proofread your personal narrative. Pay special attention to using complete sentences and correct subject-verb agreement. Use revision marks to show your changes.

Spelling Tip

Some nouns change in spelling when they are plural. Use the correct spelling when there is more than one.

person → people

scarf → scarves

hero → heroes

Present

1. **On Your Own** Make a final copy of your personal narrative. Think about how to share it with your classmates. You can read your personal narrative aloud or retell it as though you were telling it to a younger brother or sister.

Presentation Tips	
If you are the speaker . . .	**If you are the listener . . .**
Change your voice to express your feelings and to emphasize your responses to events in the story.	Listen for details that help you picture what the speaker is describing.
Use gestures if they feel natural.	Make connections to similar experiences in your own life.

2. **In a Group** Gather all the personal narratives from your class. Bind them into a class book, and work together to decide on a good title. To add interest to your own story, add computer art or scan in a photo.

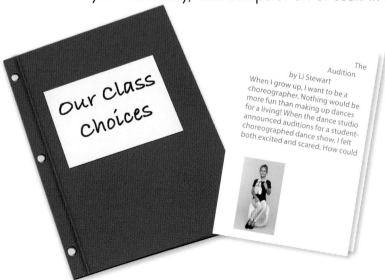

Our Class Choices

The Audition
by Li Stewart
When I grow up, I want to be a choreographer. Nothing would be more fun than making up dances for a living! When the dance studio announced auditions for a student-choreographed dance show, I felt both excited and scared. How could

BIG Question

?

How do choices affect who you are?

Talk Together

In this unit you found many answers to the **Big Question**. Now use your concept map to discuss it with the class. Think about the different choices the people and characters in the selections made. How did these choices affect their lives?

Concept Map

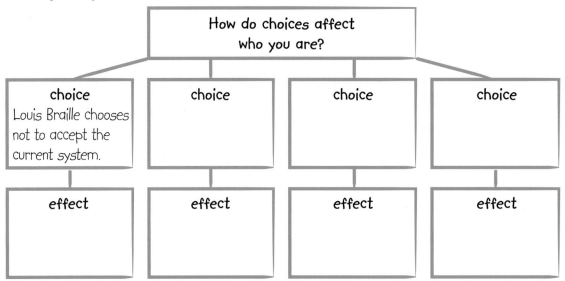

How do choices affect who you are?			
choice Louis Braille chooses not to accept the current system.	**choice**	**choice**	**choice**
effect	**effect**	**effect**	**effect**

Performance Task: Narrative

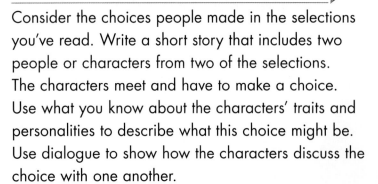

Consider the choices people made in the selections you've read. Write a short story that includes two people or characters from two of the selections. The characters meet and have to make a choice. Use what you know about the characters' traits and personalities to describe what this choice might be. Use dialogue to show how the characters discuss the choice with one another.

Checklist

Does your short story

- ✔ clearly describe the characters and setting?
- ✔ clearly develop the sequence of events?
- ✔ include transition words, descriptive details, and sensory language?

Share Your Ideas

Choose one of these ways to share your ideas about the **Big Question**.

Write It!

Write a Letter

Write a letter to thank a friend for something he or she did recently. Explain how the choices your friend made affected you personally. Include specific details about your friend's action that you appreciated.

Talk About It!

Conduct an Interview

Choose students to role-play the real people in this unit. Then prepare questions for an interview. Ask about the different choices they made and how their decisions affected their lives in positive and negative ways.

Do It!

Perform a Skit

As a class, brainstorm a list of scenarios in which a choice needs to be made. For example, *You've been secretly getting tutoring. Your best friend wants to know where you go every afternoon. Do you tell the truth?* Work with a partner to choose one scenario and prepare a skit to perform for the class.

Write It!

Write an Adventure Story

Working with a partner, use presentation software to write a short "choose your own adventure" story. Whenever your main character has to make a choice, give the readers two options. The reader clicks to make a choice for the character and then reads the effect of that choice. Remember to write an outcome for each choice you offer.

Unit 2

Survival

?
BIG
Question

What does
it take to
survive?

OSA PENINSULA, COSTA RICA
A green glass frog blending in on a leaf

Share What You Know

❶ **List** some things that help humans and animals survive.

❷ **Write** one survival method. Tape it to your partner's back.

❸ **Ask** questions. Try to guess each other's survival methods.

Describe

Look at the photo and listen to the description of the scene. Then use **Language Frames** to describe something else you notice in the photo.

Hidden Animals

I notice brown leaves scattered on a forest floor. They look dirty and ragged.

The photo shows a hidden leaf-litter toad. Its brownish skin color and ragged body shape make it look a lot like a leaf.

The toad has a stripe down its back. The stripe looks similar to the spine that goes down the center of a leaf.

These amazing adaptations hide the leaf-litter toad from predators.

Key Words

camouflage

deception

duplicate

mimic

parasite

variation

Key Words

Look at the photos and read the descriptions. Use **Key Words** and other words to talk about **variations**, or different types, of adaptations that help some animals and insects survive.

How do some organisms survive?

DECEPTION

Their adaptations use a form of **deception** to make them appear like other creatures. The eye-like spots on this butterfly make predators think it is a dangerous owl.

DUPLICATION

Their colors or patterns **duplicate**, or look very similar to, other creatures. This king snake has a pattern that looks much like the pattern of a poisonous coral snake.

king snake

robber fly

MIMICRY

Their appearance or behavior can **mimic**, or look or act like, another creature. A robber fly looks and sounds like a bumblebee.

CAMOUFLAGE

Because of **camouflage**, they can blend into their surroundings. This owl's colors, patterns, and markings help it hide in a tree.

PARASITISM

They are **parasites** who live by feeding on other creatures. This tick feeds on the blood of other animals.

Talk Together

Talk with a partner about ways that animals and insects adapt to survive. Then use the **Language Frames** from page 72 and **Key Words** to describe one of the organisms in the photos above.

Thinking Map

Main Idea and Details

Nonfiction authors often organize their writing into sections. Each section has a **main idea** and **details** that support it. When you put the main ideas of each section together, you can figure out the author's main idea for the entire selection.

MASTERS OF DISGUISE

What seems to be one thing in nature is often an imposter in disguise. Looking through the viewfinder of my camera, I have seen **plants that look like rocks, shrimp that resemble blades of grass, and flowers that up and fly away. A fly passes as a wasp; a caterpillar is disguised as a twig. Deceptions such as these allow organisms to hide from predators . . .**

"The **heading** and the **details** are both about disguises."

"The **main idea** is about how living things adapt to hide from predators."

Map and Talk

You can use a main idea chart to record important information from each section of a text. After you finish reading, analyze the main ideas of each section in order to figure out the main idea of the entire selection.

Main Idea Chart

Section Head	Important Details	Main Idea of Section
Masters of Disguise (page 80)	1. Plants look like rocks. 2. 3.	Living things adapt to hide from predators.

Talk Together

Tell a partner about two animals that have amazing abilities. Your partner creates a main idea chart that uses the animals' names as section heads and then records your details and main ideas about each animal. Then work together to determine a main idea that is true about both animals.

🔊 More Key Words

Use these words to talk about "Deception: Formula for Survival" and "Living Nightmares."

asset
noun

An **asset** is something valuable and useful. When you are hiking, a compass is a helpful **asset** that shows direction.

convince
verb

To **convince** means to make someone believe something is true. The kids will **convince** their mother to agree with their idea.

emerge
verb

To **emerge** is to appear from somewhere hidden. The sun will soon **emerge** from behind the dark clouds.

ensure
verb

To **ensure** means to make certain. This girl uses a watch to **ensure** that she meets her friend on time.

resemblance
noun

When things share a **resemblance**, they look alike. The twins share a strong **resemblance** because their features are very similar.

Talk Together

Work with a partner. Write a question using a **Key Word**. Answer the question using a different **Key Word**, if possible. Use all of the words twice.

Question: When will the animal <u>emerge</u> from hiding?

Answer: when it can <u>ensure</u> that it is safe

Learn to Visualize

When you read, do you picture how the people or scenes look? Do you imagine how things sound or smell? Sensory images are details that can help you visualize a text through all five senses: sight, sound, smell, taste, and touch.

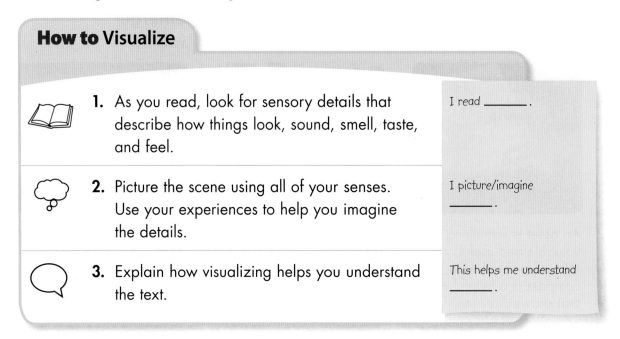

How to Visualize

1. As you read, look for sensory details that describe how things look, sound, smell, taste, and feel.

   I read _____.

2. Picture the scene using all of your senses. Use your experiences to help you imagine the details.

   I picture/imagine _____.

3. Explain how visualizing helps you understand the text.

   This helps me understand _____.

Here's how one student visualized a text about a kind of caterpillar called a looper.

Look Into the Text

When I bumped this branch inadvertently, the looper quickly became rigid in a vertical position, and **when I touched it, I found that the normally soft caterpillar had become as stiff as the adjacent twig.**

"I read **details** about a looper."

"I saw a moth that looks like an owl. I imagine a looper that looks and feels like a twig."

"This helps me understand how the looper hides."

Picturing a scene by using your senses and experiences can help you visualize what the author is describing. It can also help you better understand and remember what you read.

Talk Together

Read the scientific notebook entries and sample notes. Use **Language Frames** to visualize details as you read. Then talk with a partner about how you visualized the text.

Scientific Notebook

RAINFOREST OBSERVATIONS

Monday, May 28th

On my first day in the rainforest, I encountered a sloth resting high up in a leafy, green tree. The large, hairy mammal was hanging upside-down from its long arms and gripping a branch with its long, curved claws.

Sloths' slow speed hardly seems like a helpful **asset**, but it plays a key role in their ability to **camouflage** themselves in their surroundings. Because sloths move so slowly, small algae grow on their fur. The algae turns their grayish brown hair to a silvery green color that **ensures** they will be hidden in the rainforest canopy. ◀

> I read that sloths have "long, curved claws."
>
> I imagine claws that look like hooks!
>
> This helps me understand how sloths hold on to trees when they are hanging upside-down.

Tuesday, May 29th

At night, when the katydids **emerge**, the rainforest becomes a choir of chirping insects. Katydids are masters of **deception**. Their ability to **mimic** their surroundings can fool even a careful observer. One kind I spotted on the forest floor was a dry, dusty brown. I was **convinced** that it was another one of the leaves that crackled and crunched beneath my feet. Another **variation** had a remarkable **resemblance** to a leaf that had been eaten by insects. Its markings even **duplicated** the long, narrow veins exactly the way they look on a real leaf! ◀

Thursday, May 31st

Leafcutter ants are small but mighty creatures that work together. Larger workers use their jaws to cut pieces of leaf. Then they carry the leaves back to the nest. Smaller ants ride on the leaf pieces to keep harmful **parasites** from laying eggs on the larger workers. ◀

Today was my last day in the rainforest, but I will bring home a new appreciation for the diversity and adaptability of the amazing creatures that call the rainforest home.

◀ = a good place to visualize a detail

77

Read a Science Article

Genre

A **science article** is nonfiction. It gives facts and information about a topic related to the natural world.

Text Features

Science articles can include **photographs** that show readers what the author is explaining within the text. Photos can also present new information in a visual way. As you read, analyze the different types of information provided in the text and photos. Then combine the information in order to understand the author's ideas.

. . . the normally soft caterpillar had become as stiff as the adjacent twig.

NATIONAL
GEOGRAPHIC
EXCLUSIVE

DECEPTION

by Robert Sisson

FORMULA
FOR
SURVIVAL

MASTERS OF
DISGUISE

What seems to be one thing in nature is often **an imposter in an intriguing disguise**. Concentrating through the viewfinder of my camera, I have seen plants that look like rocks, shrimp resembling blades of grass, and flowers that up and fly away. A fly passes as a wasp; a caterpillar is disguised as a twig. **Deceptions** such as these allow organisms to hide from predators or potential victims and to increase chances of **procreation**.

Consider the two insects in the photo *(below)*. The one on the left is a species of ant that tastes bad to predatory birds. The "ant" on the right is actually a tasty plant bug whose body shape, coloring, and food sources resemble those of its unsavory neighbor. To strengthen the mirror image, it also **mimics** the ant's posture and movements.

an imposter in an intriguing disguise
something that looks like something else
procreation producing children

CAMOUFLAGE TO HUNT OR HIDE

At the edge of a desert, I was observing a crab spider on a flower of the same color, when a bee buzzed over. Failing to see the spider, the bee ended up as breakfast. Then I spotted a looper, or inchworm, under the blossom, chewing bits of petal and sticking them on its back *(left)*. As I watched, the looper inched its way up onto the center of the blossom.

The spider, alerted by the movement, climbed over the edge of the flower to look for the intruder and froze. And so did the looper and I—for the predator was standing on the camouflaged insect *(below)*. The spider finally **withdrew**, and I could breathe again.

On that one blossom I had seen two **aspects** of deception—**camouflage** to help catch prey and camouflage to escape capture.

withdrew went away
aspects variations

▶ **Before You Continue**

1. **Visualize** Use text details to imagine an organism described on page 80. How does visualizing help you understand the text?
2. **Make Comparisons** How do the looper and crab spider both have adaptations that use **deception**?

81

HIDING IN PLAIN SIGHT

Loopers usually hunch their way along with the **gait** of an **inverted U** that opens and closes. When I bumped this branch inadvertently, the looper quickly **became rigid in a vertical position** (below), and when I touched it, I found that the normally soft caterpillar had become as stiff as the **adjacent** twig.

Another looper, crawling from one twig to another, sensed a threat. It froze in a horizontal position so realistically that a predator ant strolled across it—and even stopped **en route** to **preen** (below).

Scientists have given many names to such deceptions: mimicry, cryptic coloration, camouflage, protective resemblance. They theorize that at some point **a mutant** individual is born with, for example, coloring closer to that of the leaves **on which its species browses**.

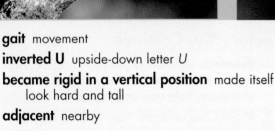

gait movement
inverted U upside-down letter *U*
became rigid in a vertical position made itself
    look hard and tall
adjacent nearby

en route on the way
preen clean itself
a mutant an unusual
on which its species browses that the
    species eats

Hungry birds, feeding on **its kin**, are likely to overlook it. And so it lives to breed and pass on the **protective adaptation**. Continuing adaptation allows the species to become a deceiver, often with more than one mode of disguise.

A successful mimic may not only look, feel, smell, and move like **its model**, but it even may **gear** its life to the same seasons in which its model operates. As mimics change to resemble their models, the models themselves are also changing. Too many good-tasting mimics in a population of untasty models would be unfortunate for both, for if predators were as likely to have a good meal as a bad one, they would begin to dine on mimic and model alike. So it is in the best interest of the model to look as unlike the mimic as possible. Call it anti-mimicry, if you wish.

its kin other insects
protective adaptation trait that keeps it safe
its model the organism it copies
gear match

▶ **Before You Continue**

1. **Summarize** Explain why a model that is copied by too many mimics might need to adapt to change its appearance.
2. **Main Idea/Details** What is the main idea of this section? What details support the main idea?

DEADLY
DECEPTION

At first, it seems a common sight, a fly prowling along a twig *(top, left)*. Suddenly the twig comes alive *(top, right)*—lashing out with clawed forelegs to **pinion** the hapless fly. My electronic flash **froze the strike**—it all took less than a tenth of a second—to show for the first time what had always before been a blur.

Discovered by Steve Montgomery of the University of Hawaii, this caterpillar of a geometrid moth strikes when tactile hairs on its body are touched. After capturing its prey, it holds the fly so the legs cannot **get purchase** in an attempt to escape.

pinion trap
froze the strike took a picture of the event
get purchase find a good grip

CHANGING DISGUISES

As a butterfly-to-be changes from an egg on a leaf to an adult, it adopts a series of disguises. After hatching, the tiger swallowtail larva survives by resembling a bird dropping *(below, lower right).*

Three molts later, it has turned green to match the leaves on which it feeds *(below, left)*. The **false eyespots** on the caterpillar's head give it a snakelike look that may frighten away predators. In **the pupal stage** it seems like just another broken twig on a tree trunk *(below, upper right).*

Three molts later After the larva's skin has changed three times
false eyespots colors that look like eyes
the pupal stage this young form

▶ **Before You Continue**

1. **Explain** How does the caterpillar of a geometrid moth catch its prey? Include text evidence in your answer.
2. **Clarify** How do the tiger swallowtail's adaptations demonstrate **variation**?

EXPERIMENTING WITH MIMICRY

Although mimicry was first scientifically described in the middle of the 19th century by Henry Walter Bates, an English **naturalist**, only recently has it been experimentally **duplicated** under natural conditions by **entomologists** Gilbert Waldbauer, Michael Jeffords, and James Sternburg of the University of Illinois.

"Other scientists have shown that the process indeed works in the laboratory," Waldbauer told me, "but demonstrating it in **the field** is a different matter. In our tests we use the day-flying male of the dark promethean moth—a natural mimic of the bad-tasting pipe-vine swallowtail butterfly.

"The promethean is shaped much like a butterfly and flies like one too. And the male is relatively easy to recapture in a trap **baited with** a female of the species.

"We paint some of the moths orange and leave dark wing markings to resemble the **unpalatable** monarch butterfly. Others we paint yellow, leaving wing markings that make them look like the tiger swallowtail, which is tastier to birds. A third batch is marked with black paint, so that their weight matches that of the other groups without altering their appearance to predators.

"We release equal numbers of all three groups in the center of a one-mile-wide circle of baited traps *(above, left)*. As we had expected, more of our mimics painted to look like unsavory models are caught in the traps undamaged, whereas the yellow ones may have beak-shaped bites taken out of their wings *(above, center, right)*.

"**Survivors** are 37 percent 'monarchs' and 39 percent 'pipe-vine swallowtails,' but only 24 percent 'tiger swallowtails.' **Batesian mimicry** does seem to be effective."

---

naturalist scientist who studied plants, animals, and insects
entomologists scientists who study insects
the field a natural setting
baited with holding

unpalatable bad-tasting
Survivors The moths that live
Batesian mimicry The kind of mimicry Bates described

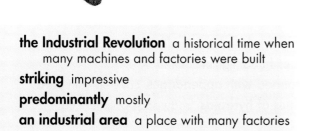

As factory smoke blackened tree trunks in England during **the Industrial Revolution**, some insects adapted to the color change. E.B. Ford of Oxford University notes that the change in moths has been **striking**.

"More than a hundred species have become **predominantly** black in England," he told me. "It is known as 'industrial melanism,' and it has also occurred in the United States."

He mentioned a study done by an associate, H.B.D. Kettlewell, using the peppered moth, which flies at night and rests exposed on tree trunks during the day. Kettlewell released equal numbers of pale and black moths in an unpolluted forest *(top, left)*. Birds took more than six times as many black moths as pale ones. But in **an industrial area**, blacks survived pale moths by four to one *(center, left)*.

The black moths are spreading for reasons other than camouflage. Genetically, most of them have become hardier—more tolerant of pollution—than the pale forms and have increased in industrial regions.

More than a century of industrialization has passed, and the British have made progress against air pollution. A sign of that success is the increase of pale moths in some industrial districts *(bottom, left)*.

the Industrial Revolution a historical time when many machines and factories were built
striking impressive
predominantly mostly
an industrial area a place with many factories

▶ **Before You Continue**

1. **Details** How does the experiment described on page 86 show that mimicry is effective? Use evidence from the text for support.

2. **Make Inferences** Why was it important for moths to adapt and change color during the Industrial Revolution?

UNDERWATER DISAPPEARING ACTS

Each time I count, I come up with a different number of grass, or phantom, shrimp in this picture *(facing page)*. Their body colors are so perfect that they seem to come and go before my eyes. There are at least 17 of them in and around the turtle grass—I think. Note that the dark green ones rest on dark green grass; brown and black ones choose dead or dying grass.

Sometimes a dark shrimp **masquerades as** a shadow under a leaf, which supports a **lighter-hued** shrimp on top.

Witness another victory at sea. A dwarf sea horse sways in the current, **festooned with appendages** that make them seem like the **plumes of hydroids** on the turtle grass to which it is anchored *(top, left)*.

masquerades as pretends to be
lighter-hued lighter-colored
festooned with appendages covered with parts
plumes of hydroids body parts of other sea
creatures

▶ **Before You Continue**

1. **Main Idea/Details** Review the details in this section. What is the main idea that they support?

2. **Use Text Features** How do the photos provide information that helps you better understand the text?

EXPERTS OF
DECEIT

Living stones are plants that survive by looking like rocks in southern Africa's deserts *(below)*. Veined wings hide a leaf katydid on a forest floor *(top, right)*.

Treehoppers march up a branch *(center, right)*, usually **aslant** like the real thorns. Some do stray onto thornless branches or face the wrong direction, but birds quickly scanning the branches usually do not spot them.

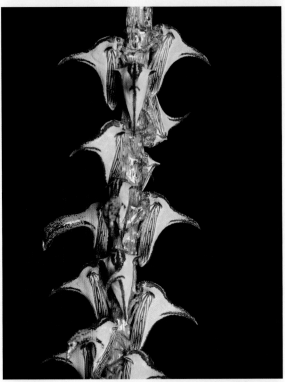

The blooms *(bottom, right)* are **larval** plant hoppers, members of a group of insects that deceive **en masse** rather than individually. **Botanists** in East Africa have picked plants adorned with the adult insects—and have been startled to see the "flowers" fly away.

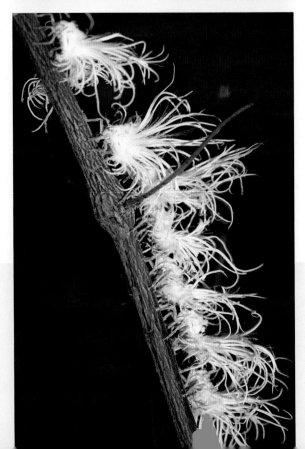

aslant shaped and placed
larval young
en masse in groups
Botanists Scientists who study plants

The feisty wasp is especially popular as a model for other insects.

An insect I photographed in Costa Rica, a mantispid, occurs there in five different color forms, and each of the five mimics a different species of paper wasp.

Study the two face-to-face insects *(below)*, and select the real wasp. Answer: the one on the right. Its companion is a hover fly, a striking mimic of the wasp.

At least one hover fly species not only looks like a wasp but also sounds like one. The **frequency of its wingbeats** is 147 a second, very close to its model's 150. Scientists call this **audio** mimicry—another adaptation in the effort to survive by deception. ❖

frequency of its wingbeats number of times it moves its wings

audio sound

▶ **Before You Continue**

1. **Make Judgments** Based on the photos and text, which organisms on page 90 have the most effective adaptations?

2. **Visualize** Based on what you know about hover flies and the description in the text, how do you imagine they sound?

Think and Respond

Key Words	
asset	ensure
camouflage	mimic
convince	parasite
deception	resemblance
duplicate	variation
emerge	

Talk About It

1. How do photos and text provide information in different ways? Choose a specific combination of photos and text from the science article, and explain how it helps you understand information.

2. Describe how both predators and prey have adaptations that **mimic** others as a way to survive. Include evidence from the text to support your description.

3. Review the section headings and evaluate whether they are helpful in determining the main idea in each section. Cite specific examples.

4. Why is **camouflage** an important **asset** to some animals in nature? Combine specific evidence from the text to form a generalization.

5. Which two organisms from the selection have adaptations that are the most similar? Which two organisms have adaptations that are the most different? Use evidence from the text to support your judgment.

6. The science article is written from the author's first-person point of view. Analyze how this affects your understanding of the information.

Write About It

Imagine that you are an organism in this selection. Write a paragraph that describes how your adaptations help you survive. Use at least three **Key Words** and sensory details to help your reader visualize your description.

As a tiger swallowtail, I **mimic** the bad-tasting pipe-vine swallowtail to **ensure** that birds will leave me alone.

Main Idea and Details

Use a main idea chart to keep track of the main idea and supporting details in each section of "Deception: Formula for Survival." Then analyze the chart to figure out the main idea of the entire science article.

Main Idea Chart

Section Head	Important Details	Main Idea of Section
Masters of Disguise (page 80)	1. Plants look like rocks. 2. 3.	Living things adapt to hide from predators.
	1.	

Use your main idea chart to summarize the main idea of each section to a partner. Then use **Key Words** as you explain how you used the information to determine the author's main idea for the entire selection.

Fluency

Practice reading with phrasing. Rate your reading.

Talk Together

Which of the insects and animals described in the article have the most effective methods of **deception** to help them survive? Use **Key Words** and cite text evidence in your discussion.

Relate Words

When you read a new word, ask yourself, "Does this new word look like a word I already know?" Some words belong in the same **word family** because they look similar and have related meanings. You can use what you know about a familiar word to help you figure out the meaning of the new word.

Word	Definition	Related Words
deception *(noun)*	the act of tricking	deceive *(verb)*, deceiver *(noun)*
duplicate *(verb)*	to copy	duplication *(noun)*
emerge *(verb)*	to appear	emerging *(adjective)*, emergence *(noun)*
mimic *(verb)*	to imitate	mimicry *(noun)*
resemblance *(noun)*	the state of being alike	resemble *(verb)*
variation *(noun)*	different type	vary *(verb)*, variety *(noun)*, variable *(noun)*

The chart above shows some related words. You already know the meaning of the verb *mimic*. What do you think the noun *mimicry* may be about?

Try It

Read the sentences. Then answer the questions.

There are many different types of butterflies in the woods. Because of this large **variety** of butterflies, it is common to find two species that **resemble** each other with similar colors and markings.

1. **What is the best definition for variety in the text?**

   A   number of different things

   B   collection of the same things

   C   similarity between things

   D   different names for things

2. **What is the best definition for resemble in the text?**

   A   to identify

   B   to differ from

   C   to look or seem like

   D   to model after

Making Connections You learned about adaptations organisms use for **deception**. Now learn about more adaptations organisms use for survival.

Genre A **science feature** is a short, nonfiction text that focuses on a specific science topic.

Living Nightmares
by Lynn Brunelle

GHOSTS

These see-through animals are masters of deception.

SPOOKFISH Deep in the ocean, you see two green dots **bobbing** in the water. The dots are eyes, but they don't seem attached to a body at all. This weird animal is called a spookfish, and it has a distinctive, ghostly, see-through head. Even though this may look scary, this see-through head is actually an adaptation, and it helps the fish survive.

A spookfish lives 800 meters (about half a mile) under the surface of the ocean, and here, its clear head and dark gray body blend into the dark water. In fact, it's hard to **spot** the fish as it floats almost motionless.

Since this fish's clear skin is like a window, the spookfish can see through it. Its round, green eyes are tucked under its skin, and they move around under its skin as it searches for prey. The fish can point its eyes forward so it can see in front of its face, and it can rotate its eyes upward to look out of the top of its head.

Since the spookfish has these unique eyes, it can spot a jellyfish floating above. Small, silver fish are trapped in the jellyfish's stinging tentacles, and the spookfish **darts** up to steal one. It swims headfirst into the tentacles, and since its eyes are safely covered by skin, they won't get stung.

bobbing bouncing up and down
spot see
darts quickly swims

▶ **Before You Continue**

1. **Main Idea/Details** What special features make the spookfish different from most other fish? Use evidence from the text to support your answer.

2. **Visualize** Which details from the text help you picture the spookfish and its habitat?

95

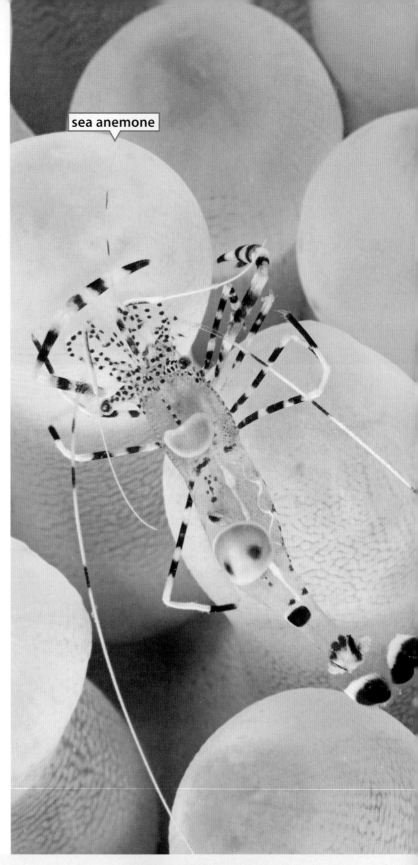

sea anemone

GHOST SHRIMP A spookfish isn't the only ghostly sea **critter**. We spot our next one on a sea anemone. It's hard to see it, because a ghost shrimp's body is mostly clear.

The shrimp uses its body as **camouflage**, so it can blend in wherever it goes. Other critters see only the surface on which the shrimp is standing, so the shrimp remains safely hidden from predators.

Being clear only works as long as the ghost shrimp doesn't eat. When the shrimp **nibbles algae**, its food shows through its transparent body.

critter animal; creature
nibbles algae eats small plants

GLASS FROG Another ghostly creature lives in a rain forest; it makes a squeaky "peep" sound. The sound seems like it's coming from a pale, green leaf, but it looks as if there is no critter on the leaf.

Suddenly, a bump on the leaf wiggles, and it's a frog. Like the other ghostly creatures you've read about, this frog is a master of disguise. Because it blends in with the leaf, it is almost invisible until it moves. It's not the same color as the leaf, however. Like the shrimp, a glass frog blends in because it has almost no color at all.

The skin on its belly is clear, and its back is pale green. The bright green of the leaf shines right through this frog; it makes the frog look like part of the leaf. This **resemblance** helps the glass frog hide from its predators.

Most of the time, this frog blends in. Flip the frog over, however, and you can see its insides. You can see its heart pumping blood and watch food squeeze through its guts.

▶ **Before You Continue**

1. **Make Inferences** What might happen if a ghost shrimp is eating when a predator swims by? Why?

2. **Explain** Why is the adaptation of **camouflage** so important to the ghost shrimp and the glass frog?

ZOMBIES

Some organisms use mind control to get ahead.

ZOMBIE ANT A line of ants marches through a rain forest. One by one, the ants climb a tree trunk to head up to their warm, dry nest. Suddenly, one ant stumbles out of line, twitches a little, and then drops to the ground. Something is wrong because these ants usually never step out of line.

Near the ground, the ant finds a leaf. It crawls under the leaf where it's damp and shady, and then it bites into the leaf. Suddenly, the ant's jaws lock, and it can't let go or even move. The ant hangs from the leaf, slowly dying. This ant is acting odd for a scary reason—because it's a zombie. You can't see it, but a killer now controls the ant.

The ant was fine days earlier, until it picked up a tiny **hitchhiker** smaller than a grain of sand. The hitchhiker was a **fungus spore**, and it dug its way into the ant's body. Even though the ant doesn't feel a thing, the **parasite** goes to work inside the ant's body. It reproduces and spreads, and it eventually takes over the ant's brain. The fungus inside of it makes the ant find a damp, shady place, because that's where a fungus grows best.

The fungus sprouts from the ant's head, and this makes the ant look like it is growing antennae. By now, the ant is dead, but the fungus keeps growing until it explodes. These new splattered spores will attach themselves to other ants to make new zombies.

get ahead get what they need
hitchhiker traveler
fungus spore tiny intruder

ZOMBIE SNAIL Fungi aren't the only zombie masters. A kind of flatworm **hijacks** a snail, and the results aren't pretty. Like the fungus, the worm is a parasite. As the snail slowly crawls across the ground looking for bird droppings to eat, it has no idea that flatworm eggs are in the droppings.

When the snail eats the droppings, the flatworm eggs hatch inside the snail. When the young flatworms start to grow, they move into the snail's eyestalks, which are the long stems that hold the snail's eyes. The snail's eyestalks start to grow bigger and more colorful.

Because its body has been taken over, the snail starts acting very odd. Usually, it hides in the shadows to avoid predators. Now, the flatworms have taken over its brain, and they make the snail crawl into wide-open spaces.

The snail wriggles its swollen eyestalks; they look like juicy caterpillars. A bird sees the moving eyestalks, swoops in, and rips the eyestalks off the snail. The doomed snail crawls away, but inside the bird's gut, the flatworms finish growing. They lay eggs, and these eggs may become food for more snails.

hijacks takes over

▶ **Before You Continue**

1. **Compare** How do the fungus spore and flatworm's adaptations help them survive?
2. **Author's Viewpoint** How does the author view the **parasites** in this section? Cite evidence to support your response.

DEVILS

These critters use scary looks and sounds to survive.

TASMANIAN DEVIL Just after midnight, a howl rises from a forest in Australia. A fearsome growl answers it, and then there's a scream. Sharp teeth **flash**, and fur flies. This forest sounds haunted, but these sounds are just caused by two Tasmanian devils fighting over a dead animal.

These scavengers eat dead animals, and it's best to stay out of their way. They may weigh only about 8 kg (about 17 pounds), but they have one of the most powerful bites of any mammal. Their teeth can crush bones and rip apart fur and guts.

These devils fight over food, they **brawl** over space, they battle for mates, and they attack predators. When Tasmanian devils fight, their ears turn bright red. Then they spray a stinky smell, **gnash** their teeth, and scream. They act devilish in order to survive.

THORNY DEVIL A second kind of devil lives in a desert in Australia. Spikes stick out from its body, and they look like sharp thorns. Meet the thorny devil lizard. Its prickly outside makes it look dangerous, but its looks are an interesting adaptation.

At dawn, the lizard rubs against a bush that is covered in dew. Dew runs down its spikes and into tiny grooves on its skin. The grooves lead to the lizard's mouth, allowing the lizard to drink the dew. Now it can survive another **devilishly** hot day in the desert.

Despite its looks, only ants should fear the thorny devil. It licks them up with its tongue and crunches them with its teeth. In fact, it can eat as many as 3,000 ants in a single meal.

flash bite and tear
brawl fight
gnash grind
devilishly horribly

HICKORY HORNED DEVIL

Our last creepy critter, the hickory horned devil, crawls along a branch high in a tree. This devil is a caterpillar, and it can grow up to 15 cm long. When it **rears up**, nearly a dozen spiky red and black horns stick out of its head. It shakes its head and buzzes. This creepy critter looks and acts devilish in order to scare away predators and get back to what it does best—munching tree leaves.

From devils to zombie masters to ghosts, these critters may seem like living nightmares. Some seem to vanish, and others howl horribly or force victims to grow freaky body parts. Their adaptations may make them look and act scary, but each adaptation helps them survive. ❖

rears up stands up straight

▶ **Before You Continue**

1. **Use Text Features** How do the photographs present information in a different way than the text? Cite specific examples.
2. **Interpret** Why does this science feature describe these creatures as "living nightmares"?

Key Words

asset	ensure
camouflage	mimic
convince	parasite
deception	resemblance
duplicate	variation
emerge	

Compare Texts

The selections, "Deception: Formula for Survival" and "Living Nightmares" both tell about ways that animals survive. Think about the main idea of each text and the details the authors include. Then work with a partner to complete the chart below. Use the information to evaluate how the two selections present information about the same scientific topic.

Comparison Chart

	"Deception: Formula for Survival"	"Living Nightmares"
Main Idea of Selection	Some species _____ .	Some species _____ .
Details that Support the Main Idea	1. 2. 3.	1. 2. 3.
Text Features		

Talk Together

How do the authors of "Deception: Formula for Survival" and "Living Nightmares" help you understand how species are adapted for survival? Use **Key Words** and text evidence to talk about your ideas.

Subject and Object Pronouns

A **pronoun** is a word that takes the place of a noun. The type of pronoun to use depends on how it is used in a sentence.

Grammar Rules Subject and Object Pronouns	
Use a **subject pronoun** in place of a **noun** as the subject of a sentence.	The **jellyfish** floats by. **It** does not see the transparent spookfish.
The subject pronouns are *I*, *you*, *he*, *she*, *it*, *we*, and *they*.	The **eyes** of a spookfish are odd. **They** are tucked under the skin.
Use an **object pronoun** in place of a **noun** after an **action verb**.	Small, silver **fish** are trapped. The spookfish **eats** **them**.
Also use an **object pronoun** in place of a **noun** after a **preposition**.	The **tentacles** sting, but the spookfish swims **through** **them**.
The object pronouns are *me*, *you*, *him*, *her*, *it*, *us*, and *them*.	

Read Subject and Object Pronouns

Writers want to avoid repeating the same words too many times, so they use subject and object pronouns to take the place of some repeated nouns. Read this passage from "Living Nightmares." Identify the subject and object pronouns. How do they make the writing smooth and easy to read?

> Despite its looks, only ants should fear the thorny devil. It licks them up with its tongue and crunches them with its teeth.
> In fact, it can eat as many as 3,000 ants in a single meal.

Write Subject and Object Pronouns

Write a short paragraph about one of the creatures in "Living Nightmares." Include at least two subject and object pronouns. Then compare your work with a partner's.

Language Frames

- For example, _____ .
- In addition _____ .
- Not only _____ , but _____ .

Elaborate

Look at the photo and listen to the presentation. Then use **Language Frames** to elaborate on an important detail about survival from the presentation.

Survival Basics

When it comes to survival, humans and animals share many similarities. For example, all living creatures require food and water in order to survive. Without these two basic things, most living things would die within days. In addition to essential nutrients, humans and animals also require shelter to keep them safe from different kinds of danger, such as severe weather and predators. Not only do humans build their own homes, but many animals build complicated shelters, too, such as birds that build nests and beavers that construct dams. All living things share the same basic needs, and all have found amazing ways to adapt and survive.

Science Vocabulary

🔊 # Key Words

Key Words
exhaust
necessity
overcome
reliance
resourceful

Look at the illustration and read the text. Use **Key Words** and other words to talk about how you can **overcome**, or conquer, the challenges in nature.

Tips for Hiking

When you are hiking, the most important **necessity** that you must have is water. Take small sips so that you do not **exhaust**, or use up, your water supply too quickly.

TIP 1

If you have to camp overnight, you can be creative and **resourceful** by making a shelter out of the materials around you.

TIP 2

TIP 3

Most hikers wear sturdy boots or shoes. Some also have a **reliance** on tools, such as walking sticks. They need these tools to stay safe on the trail.

Talk Together

Talk with a partner about the three safety tips above. Then give another safety tip. Use the **Language Frames** from page 104 and **Key Words** to elaborate on your idea with more information and details.

Character

Most stories focus on a main **character** who has a problem or goal. To understand the character, think about the person's:

- **motives:** reasons why the character does or says something.

- **actions:** what the character says and does.

As you read the story, look for text evidence that helps you understand the main character.

Look Into the Text

> Here I am and that is nowhere. With his mind opened and thoughts happening, it all tried to come in with a rush, all of what had occurred and he could not take it. The whole thing turned into a confused jumble that made no sense. So he fought it down and tried to take one thing at a time . . .
>
> My name is Brian Robeson and I am thirteen years old and I am alone in the north woods of Canada.
>
> All right, he thought, that's simple enough.

"Brian's **motive** is that he is confused and scared. He needs to figure out what is happening."

"His **actions** are to calm down and think clearly."

Map and Talk

A character chart can help you analyze details about a character's motives and actions to help you learn more about the character.

Character Chart

Character: Brian Robeson	
Motives	**Actions**
wants to figure out what is happening	

Talk Together

Tell a partner about a time you had to do something important. What motivated you? What actions did you take? Describe the experience while a partner completes a character chart about the experience and explains something that it shows about you.

🔊 More Key Words

Use these words to talk about "Hatchet" and "Survival Stories: The Girl Who Fell from the Sky."

concentrate
verb

When you **concentrate**, you give all of your attention to something. The boy must **concentrate** when he glues the tiny pieces together.

intense
adjective

Something that is **intense** is very strong. The **intense** wind made the tree tops bend over.

motivation
noun

Motivation is the reason for doing something. My **motivation** for studying is to get good grades.

resilience
noun

When you show **resilience**, you can recover from or adapt to difficult situations. Plants show **resilience** by growing in places with little or no soil.

resolve
verb

When you **resolve** to do something, you reach a decision about it. After seeing the litter, the kids **resolve** to pick up trash once a week.

Talk Together

With a partner, make an Expanded Meaning Map for each **Key Word**.

Definition	Characteristics
to get better	strong successful

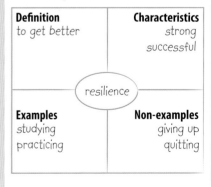
resilience

Examples	Non-examples
studying practicing	giving up quitting

Learn to Visualize

As you read, use details in the text to create mental images, or pictures in your mind. When you combine these images with your own experience, you react to what you read. These reactions, or emotional responses, can deepen your understanding of the text.

How to Visualize

📖	**1.** As you read, notice words and phrases that create images in your mind.	I read _____ .
💬	**2.** Describe what you "see" and "hear" in your mind.	I see/hear _____ .
💭	**3.** Combine these mental images of the text with your own experience to identify how you feel. Consider how identifying your emotional responses helps you understand the text.	I feel _____ . I understand _____ .

Here's how one student visualized a text and responded.

Look Into the Text

"I'm hungry." He said it aloud. In normal tones at first, then louder and louder until he was yelling it. "I'm hungry, I'm hungry, I'm hungry!"

When he stopped there was sudden silence, not just from him but the clicks and blurps and bird sounds of the forest as well. The noise of his voice had startled everything and it was quiet. He looked around, listened with his mouth open, and realized that in all his life he had never heard silence before. **Complete silence.** There had always been some sound, some kind of sound.

"I read **details** about silence."

"I hear the total silence in the forest."

"I remember feeling silence like that, so I feel worried about Brian. I understand how scared and lonely he must feel."

Visualizing and forming emotional responses to the text can help you relate to the story and gain a deeper understanding of what you've read.

Read the journal entry and sample notes. Use **Language Frames** to visualize and form emotional responses as you read. Then talk with a partner about how you responded to the text.

Journal Entry

A Backcountry Adventure

Sunday, July 10th

We are back from our three-day camping trip to the Shenandoah Valley. Mom and Dad had been concerned about our family's **reliance** on computers, cell phones, and video games for entertainment. So they decided a camping trip would help us **overcome** our dependence on electronic devices. I knew we'd have to be **resilient** in order to find a way to survive without the comforts of home.

When you camp in the backcountry, you have to carry all of your supplies with you. We could only bring **necessities** that we needed to survive, such as food, clothes, a camp stove, fuel, rope, a map, and a water container. At first, I was surprised that we weren't bringing bottled water with us. Then my heavy, overstuffed backpack made me realize we'd soon **exhaust** any supply we could carry. Instead, we'd have to be **resourceful** and boil or filter water from nearby streams. ◄

Our first day in the wilderness was incredible. We scrabbled up rocky paths and waded in an ice-cold stream that made my feet tingle. Fragrant wildflowers waved their colorful petals at us. I felt like I had stepped into a dreamy landscape painting. After all that exercise, an **intense** hunger burned in the pit of my stomach. Mom's homemade trail mix had never tasted so good. ◄

At night, the darkness seemed like a black curtain had been dropped over us. I tried to read with a flashlight, but I couldn't **concentrate**. I finally fell asleep to a chorus of chirping crickets.

By our last day, I had blistered feet and bug-bitten arms. I was ready to go home. I couldn't wait to play video games. But a funny thing happened. Soon after I started my favorite game, I lost the **motivation** to continue. I headed outside to get some fresh air. Mom and Dad's plan had worked after all. Right then I **resolved** to spend more time in the great outdoors. ◄

I read about the supplies the family needs to carry.

I see big, heavy packs bulging with food and equipment.

I feel sympathy for the family because each person has to carry a heavy load.

I understand why the family could only pack necessities.

◄ = a good place to form mental images

Read an Adventure Story

Genre

An **adventure story** tells about events that are dangerous or exciting. In this fictional adventure story, the author describes how a character reacts to his experiences and overcomes obstacles.

Point of View

Point of view describes how a story is told. In **third-person point of view**, a narrator who is not a character tells the story. When the third-person point of view is **omniscient**, the narrator knows everything about the story's events, including all of the character's thoughts and feelings.

The narrator describes the character's actions and thoughts.

> Brian rubbed his stomach. The hunger had been there but something else—fear, pain—had held it down. Now, with the thought of the burger, the emptiness roared at him.

from HATCHET

by Gary Paulsen

ILLUSTRATED BY JULIANA KOLESOVA

▶ **Set a Purpose**
Find out about a challenge
that a 13-year-old boy
must **overcome** in the forest.

Here I am and that is nowhere. With his mind **opened** and thoughts happening, it all tried to come in with a rush, all of what had occurred and he could not **take it**. The whole thing turned into a confused jumble that made no sense. So he **fought it down** and tried to take one thing at a time.

He had been flying north to visit his father for a couple of months in the summer, and the pilot had had a heart attack and had died, and the plane had crashed somewhere in the Canadian north woods but he did not know how far they had flown or in what direction or where he was . . .

opened able to think
take it understand it all
fought it down made himself calm down

Slow down, he thought. Slow down more.

My name is Brian Robeson, and I am thirteen years old, and I am alone in the north woods of Canada.

All right, he thought, that's simple enough.

I was flying to visit my father and the plane crashed and sank in a lake.

There, keep it that way. Short thoughts.

I do not know where I am.

Which doesn't mean much. More to the point, *they* do not know where I am—*they* meaning anybody who might be wanting to look for me. The searchers.

They would look for him, look for the plane. His father and mother would be **frantic**. They would tear the world apart to find him. Brian had seen searches on the news, seen movies about lost planes. When a plane went down they **mounted extensive searches** and almost always they found the plane within a day or two. Pilots all filed flight plans—a detailed plan for where and when they were going to fly, with all the courses explained. They would come, they would look for him. The searchers would get government planes and cover both sides of the flight plan filed by the pilot and search until they found him.

Maybe even today. They might come today. This was the second day after the crash. No. Brian frowned. Was it the first day or the second day? They had gone down in the afternoon and he had spent the whole night **out cold**. So this was the first real day. But they could still come today. They would have started the search immediately when Brian's plane did not arrive.

frantic very afraid and worried
mounted extensive searches sent many people
  to help
out cold unconscious

Yeah, they would probably come today.

Probably come in here with amphibious planes, small bushplanes with floats that could land right here on the lake and pick him up and take him home.

Which home? The father home or the mother home. He stopped the thinking. It didn't matter. Either on to his dad or back to his mother. Either way he would probably be home by late night or early morning, home where he could sit down and eat a large, cheesy, juicy burger with tomatoes and double fries with ketchup and a thick chocolate shake.

And there came hunger.

Brian rubbed his stomach. The hunger had been there but something else—fear, pain—had held it down. Now, with the thought of the burger, the emptiness **roared at him**. He could not believe the hunger, had never felt it this way. The lake water had filled his stomach but left it hungry, and now it demanded food, screamed for food.

And there was, he thought, absolutely nothing to eat.
Nothing.

What did they do in the movies when they got stranded like this? Oh, yes, the hero usually found some kind of plant that he knew was good to eat and that took care of it. Just ate the plant until he was full or used some kind of cute trap to catch an animal and cook it over a **slick** little fire and pretty soon he had a full eight-course meal.

The trouble, Brian thought, looking around, was that all he could see was grass and brush. There was nothing obvious to eat, and aside from about a million birds and the beaver, he hadn't seen animals to trap and cook; and even if he got one somehow, he didn't have any matches, so he couldn't have a fire . . .

roared at him was **intense**
slick perfect

Nothing.

It kept coming back to that. He had nothing.

Well, almost nothing. As a matter of fact, he thought, I don't know what I've got or haven't got. Maybe I should try and figure out just how I **stand**. It will give me something to do—keep me from thinking of food. Until they come to find me.

Brian had once had an English teacher, a guy named Perpich, who was always talking about being positive, thinking positive, **staying on top of things**. That's how Perpich had put it—stay positive and stay on top of things. Brian thought of him now—wondered how to stay positive and stay on top of this. All Perpich would say is that I have to get motivated. He was always telling kids to get motivated.

Brian changed position so he was sitting on his knees. He reached into his pockets and took out everything he had and laid it on the grass in front of him.

It was **pitiful** enough. A quarter, three dimes, a nickel, and two pennies. A fingernail clipper. A billfold with a twenty dollar bill— "In case you get stranded at the airport in some small town and have to buy food," his mother had said—and **some odd** pieces of paper.

stand am doing
staying on top of things keeping focused on what
    you need to do
pitiful sad
some odd a few

And on his belt, somehow still there, the hatchet his mother had given him. He had forgotten it and now reached around and took it out and put it in the grass. There was a touch of rust already forming on the cutting edge of the blade and he rubbed it off with his thumb.

That was it.

He frowned. No, wait—if he was going to **play the game, might as well play it right**. Perpich would tell him to quit messing around. Get motivated. Look at *all* of it, Robeson.

He had on a pair of good tennis shoes, now almost dry. And socks. And jeans and underwear and a thin leather belt and a T-shirt with a windbreaker so torn it hung on him in tatters.

And a watch. He had a digital watch still on his wrist but it was broken from the crash—the little screen blank—and he took it off and almost threw it away but stopped the hand motion and lay the watch on the grass with the rest of it.

There. That was it.

No, wait. One other thing. Those were all the things he had, but he also had himself. Perpich used to **drum that into them**—"You are your most valuable asset. Don't forget that. *You* are the best thing you have."

play the game, might as well play it right
survive, he had to do his best
drum that into them always remind them

▶ **Before You Continue**
1. **Paraphrase** What lessons has Brian learned from Perpich?
2. **Point of View** Identify examples in which the narrator includes Brian's thoughts. How does this help you understand the story?

▶ **Predict**
Will Brian have the **resilience**
he needs to survive?

Brian looked around again. I wish you were here, Perpich. I'm hungry and I'd trade everything I have for a hamburger.

"I'm hungry." He said it aloud. In normal tones at first, then louder and louder until he was yelling it. "I'm hungry, I'm hungry, I'm hungry!"

When he stopped there was sudden silence, not just from him but the clicks and blurps and bird sounds of the forest as well. The noise of his voice had startled everything and it was quiet. He looked around, listened with his mouth open, and realized that in all his life he had never heard silence before. Complete silence. There had always been some sound, some kind of sound.

It lasted only a few seconds, but it was so **intense** that it seemed to become part of him. Nothing. There was no sound. Then the bird started again, and some kind of buzzing insect, and then a chattering and a cawing, and soon there was the same background of sound.

Which left him still hungry.

Of course, he thought, putting the coins and the rest back in his pocket and the hatchet in his belt—of course if they come tonight or even if they take as long as tomorrow the hunger is no big thing. People have gone for many days without food as long as they've got water. Even if they don't come until late tomorrow I'll be all right. Lose a little weight, maybe, but the first hamburger and a malt and fries will bring it right back.

A mental picture of a hamburger, the way they showed it in the television commercials, thundered into his thoughts. Rich colors, the meat juicy and hot . . .

He pushed the picture away. So even if they didn't find him until tomorrow, he thought, he would be all right. He had plenty of water, although he wasn't sure if it was good and clean or not.

He sat again by the tree, his back against it. There was a thing bothering him. He wasn't quite sure what it was but it kept chewing at the edge of his thoughts. Something about the plane and the pilot that would change things . . .

Ahh, there it was—the moment when the pilot had his heart attack his right foot had jerked down on the rudder pedal and the plane had **slewed** sideways. What did that mean? Why did that keep coming into his thinking that way, nudging and pushing?

It means, a voice in his thoughts said, that they might not be coming for you tonight or even tomorrow. When the pilot pushed the rudder pedal the plane had jerked to the side and **assumed** a new course. Brian could not remember how much it had pulled around, but it wouldn't have had to be much because after that, with the pilot dead, Brian had flown for hour after hour on the new course.

Well away from the flight plan the pilot had filed. Many hours, at maybe 160 miles an hour. Even if it was only a little off course, with that speed and time Brian might now be sitting several hundred miles off to the side of the recorded flight plan.

And they would probably search most heavily at first along the flight plan course. They might go out to the side a little, but he could easily be three, four hundred miles to the side. He could not know, could not think of how far he might have flown wrong because he didn't know the original course and didn't know how much they had pulled sideways.

Quite a bit—that's how he remembered it. Quite a jerk to the side. It pulled his head over sharply when the plane had swung around.

They might not find him for two or three days. He felt his heartbeat increase as the fear started. The thought was there but he fought it down for a time, pushed it away, then it exploded out.

They might not find him for a long time.

slewed turned
assumed taken

And the next thought was there as well, that they might never find him, but that was panic and he fought it down and tried to stay positive. They searched hard when a plane went down, they used many men and planes and they would go to the side, they would know he was off from the flight path, he had talked to the man on the radio, they would somehow know . . .

It would be all right.

They would find him. Maybe not tomorrow, but soon. Soon. Soon.

They would find him soon.

Gradually, like sloshing oil his thoughts settled back and the panic was gone. Say they didn't come for two days—no, say they didn't come for three days, even push that to four days—he could live with that. He would have to live with that. He didn't want to think of them taking longer. But say four days. He had to do something. He couldn't just sit at the bottom of this tree and stare down at the lake for four days.

And nights. He was in deep woods and didn't have any matches, couldn't make a fire. There were large things in the woods. There were wolves, he thought, and bears—other things. In the dark he would be in the open here, just sitting at the bottom of a tree.

He looked around suddenly, felt the hair on the back of his neck go up. Things might be looking at him right now, waiting for him—waiting for dark so they could move in and take him.

He fingered the hatchet at his belt. It was the only weapon he had, but it was something.

He had to have some kind of shelter. No, make that more: He had to have some kind of shelter and he had to have something to eat.

He pulled himself to his feet and jerked the back of his shirt down before the mosquitos could get at it. He had to do something to help himself.

I have to get motivated, he thought, remembering Perpich. Right now I'm all I've got. I have to do something. ❖

▶ **Before You Continue**

1. **Character** What motivates Brian to stop panicking and take action?
2. **Visualize** Which details help you picture Brian's actions and feelings? How do they help you understand the story?

Meet the Author

GARY PAULSEN

Much of Gary Paulsen's work is inspired by his real-life adventures. When he was just 14, he traveled with the circus. He spent summers working on ranches and ships. Becoming independent at a young age became a major theme in many of his novels, including *Hatchet* and its four sequels. Paulsen also competed twice in the Iditarod, a brutal 1,180-mile Alaskan dog sled race that inspired him to write an award-winning novel called *Dogsong*.

Thanks to Paulsen's writing, his readers are invited to join in his experiences, too.

Paulsen says that writers should write something every day. "Even if you wind up deleting everything you've written, at least keep your hand moving and the words flowing." With luck—and hard work—his readers could go on to write about their own real-life adventures.

Writer's Craft

In "Hatchet," the author uses a combination of long and short sentences to convey Brian's sense of helplessness and fear: "I was flying to visit my father and the plane crashed and sank in a lake. There, keep it that way. Short thoughts."

Write a brief description of a scary situation. Use a variety of sentence lengths to convey your mood. Think about how you can share your personal thoughts in your description like Brian in the novel.

Think and Respond

Key Words

concentrate	overcome
exhaust	reliance
intense	resilience
motivation	resolve
necessity	resourceful

Talk About It 💬

1. "Hatchet" is an adventure story. Use specific examples from the text to describe Brian's situation and the obstacles he must **overcome**.

2. Identify the **necessities** that Brian needs in order to survive in the wilderness. Elaborate on the dangers Brian faces and how he should deal with them.

3. What causes Brian to change his attitude about waiting for rescue? Use evidence from the text to explain the change and what this shows about Brian.

4. How does Brian show **resilience** during his ordeal? Cite evidence from the text to support your answer.

5. Review Brian's actions. Based on what you have read and what you know about survival, which of Brian's decisions is the best example of being **resourceful**? Why?

6. How would Brian's story be different if it were told from Brian's viewpoint instead of a third-person narrator? Choose a specific scene from the selection and analyze how the point of view affects the story.

Write About It ✏️

Imagine that Brian has been rescued. Write a speech in which Brian describes and elaborates on his experiences. Use at least three **Key Words**.

> *Well, at first I was **overcome** with panic. I couldn't believe all the things that had happened to me in such a short time.*

Analyze Character

Use a character chart to organize your thoughts about Brian. Look back at the story to see what Brian does and why he does it.

Character Chart

Character: Brian Robeson	
Motives	**Actions**
wants to figure out what is happening	stops panicking and tries to think clearly

Use your character chart to describe Brian to a partner. Explain what his actions and **motivations** show you about his character. Use **Key Words**.

Fluency

Practice reading with expression. Rate your reading.

Talk Together

What qualities are the key to survival in the wilderness? Include **Key Words** and examples from Brian's experiences in "Hatchet" as you discuss your ideas with a small group.

Word Work

Shades of Meaning

Good writers choose words that say exactly what they mean. Many words have **synonyms**, or words that have similar meanings. You can consult a thesaurus for synonyms. Then arrange the words on a synonym scale to show how they relate.

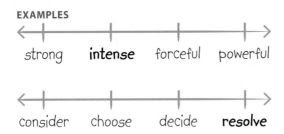

EXAMPLES

strong · **intense** · forceful · powerful

consider · choose · decide · **resolve**

According to the synonym scale above, the word *consider* is not as strong a word as *resolve*. What is another word you could add to the scale?

Try It

Read the sentence. Then answer the two-part question. First, answer part A. Then answer part B.

> That night, the storm completely destroyed Brian's shelter, ruined his supplies, and threatened his life.

PART A

1. **What is most likely the author's reason for describing the shelter as "completely destroyed"?**

   A to give details about Brian's shelter

   B to show the strength of the storm

   C to show how to survive a storm

   D to explain why Brian has a shelter

PART B

2. **Which synonym best describes the storm in part A?**

   A strong

   B intense

   C forceful

   D powerful

Making Connections You read a story about a boy who must survive in a forest. Now read the true account of a teenager who survived a real-life plane crash.

Genre In a **personal narrative**, an author tells a story about true events from his or her life.

from Survival Stories:

The Girl Who Fell from the Sky

by Juliane Koepcke Diller

▲ Juliane Koepcke Diller in the Peruvian rain forest

The first half of the hour-long flight from Lima to Pucallpa is uneventful. We're served a sandwich and a drink for breakfast. Ten minutes later, as the **flight attendants** begin to clean up, we fly into a huge thunderstorm.

Suddenly, daylight turns to night and lightning flashes from all directions. People gasp as the plane shakes violently. Bags, wrapped gifts, and clothing fall from overhead lockers. Sandwich trays soar through the air, and half-finished drinks spill onto passengers' heads. People scream and cry.

"Hopefully this goes all right," my mother says nervously.

flight attendants workers on the airplane

▶ **Before You Continue**

1. **Setting** How does the setting of the narrative drastically change? Use evidence from the text to support your answer.
2. **Make Connections** What is a connection that helps you understand Diller's feelings about this experience?

125

I see a blinding white light over the right wing. I don't know whether it's a flash of lightning or an explosion. I lose all sense of time. The airplane begins to **nosedive**. From my seat in the back, I can see down the aisle into the cockpit.

My ears, my head, my whole body are filled with the deep roar of the plane. Over everything, I hear my mother say calmly, "Now it's all over."

We're falling fast. People's shouts and the roar of the turbines suddenly go silent.

My mother is no longer at my side, and I'm no longer in the plane. I'm still strapped into my seat on the bench, at an altitude of about 10,000 feet. I'm alone. And I'm falling.

My free fall is quiet. I see nothing around me. The seat belt squeezes my belly so tight that I can't breathe. Before I feel fear, I lose consciousness.

When I **come to**, I'm upside down, still falling, the Peruvian rain forest spinning slowly toward me. The densely packed treetops remind me of broccoli. I see everything as if through a fog before I pass out again.

When I regain consciousness, I've landed in the middle of the jungle. My seat belt is unfastened, so I must have woken up at some point. I've crawled deeper into the sheltering back of the three-seat bench that was fastened to me when I fell from the sky. Wet and muddy, I lie there for the rest of the day and night.

I will never forget the image I see when I open my eyes the next morning: The crowns of the giant trees above me are **suffused** with golden light, bathing everything in a green glow. I feel abandoned, helpless, and utterly alone. My mother's seat beside me is empty.

I can't stand up. I hear the soft ticking of my watch but can't read the time. I can't see straight. I realize that my left eye is swollen shut; I can see only through a narrow slit in my right eye. My glasses have disappeared, but I finally manage to read the time.

It's 9 a.m. I feel dizzy again and lie exhausted on the rain forest floor. After a while, I manage to rise to my knees, but I feel so dizzy that I immediately lie back down. I try again, and eventually I'm able to hold myself in that position. I touch my right collarbone; it's clearly broken. I find a deep gash on my left **calf**, which looks as if it has been cut by a rough metal edge. Strangely, it's not bleeding.

I get down on all fours and crawl around, searching for my mother. I call her name, but only the voices of the jungle answer me.

nosedive fall toward the ground
come to wake up
suffused filled
calf lower leg

katydid

For someone who has never been in the rain forest, it can seem threatening. Huge trees cast mysterious shadows. Water drips constantly. The rain forest often has a musty smell from the plants that intertwine and ramble, grow and decay.

Insects rule the jungle, and I encounter them all: ants, beetles, butterflies, grasshoppers, mosquitoes. A certain type of fly will lay eggs under the skin or in wounds. Stingless wild bees like to cling to hair.

Luckily, I'd lived in the jungle long enough as a child to be acquainted with the bugs and other creatures that scurry, rustle, whistle, and snarl. There was almost nothing my parents hadn't taught me about the jungle. I only had to find this knowledge in my **concussion-fogged** head.

Suddenly I'm seized by an **intense** thirst. Thick drops of water sparkle on the leaves around me, and I lick them up. I walk in small circles around my seat, aware of how quickly you can lose your **orientation** in the jungle. I memorize the location and markings of one tree to **keep my bearings**.

concussion-fogged injured and confused
orientation sense of direction
keep my bearings remember where I am

▶ **Before You Continue**

1. **Visualize** What words does the author use to help you picture the forest? How does this make you feel about her situation?
2. **Point of View** How does the author's first-person point of view help you understand the story?

I find no trace of the crash. No wreckage, no people. But I do discover a bag of candy and eat a piece.

I hear the hum of airplane engines overhead. I look up, but the trees are too dense: There's no way I can make myself noticeable here. A feeling of powerlessness **overcomes** me. I have to get out of the thick of the forest so that rescuers can see me. Soon the engines' hum fades away.

I hear the dripping, tinkling, gurgle of water that I hadn't noticed before. Nearby I find a spring, feeding a tiny **rivulet**. This fills me with hope. Not only have I found water to drink, but I'm convinced that this little stream will lead the way to my rescue.

I try to follow the rivulet closely, but there are often tree trunks lying across it, or dense **undergrowth** blocks my way. Little by little, the rivulet grows wider and turns into a stream, which is partly dry, so that I can easily walk beside the water. Around six o'clock it gets dark, and I look in the streambed for a protected spot where I can spend the night. I eat another candy.

rivulet stream of running water
undergrowth plant life

December 28, my watch, a gift from my grandmother, stops for good, so I try to count the days as I go. The stream turns into a larger stream, then finally into a small river. Since it's the rainy season, there's barely any fruit to pick, and I've sucked on my last candy. I don't have a knife to use to **hack palm hearts** out of the stems of the palm trees. Nor can I catch fish or cook roots. I don't dare eat anything else. Much of what grows in the jungle is poisonous, so I keep my hands off what I don't recognize. But I do drink a great deal of water from the stream.

Despite counting, I mix up the days. On December 29 or 30, the fifth or sixth day of my trek, I hear a buzzing, groaning sound that immediately turns my **apathetic** mood into **euphoria**. It's the unmistakable call of a hoatzin, a subtropical bird that nests exclusively near open stretches of water—where people settle! At home in Panguana, I heard this call often.

With new impetus, I walk faster, following the sound. Finally, I'm standing on the bank of a large river, but there's **not a soul** in sight. I hear planes in the distance, but as time passes, the noise fades. I believe that they've given up, having rescued all the passengers except me.

Intense anger overcomes me. How can the pilots turn around, now that I've finally reached an open stretch of water after all these days? Soon, my anger gives way to a terrible **despair**.

But I don't give up. Where there is a river, people cannot be far away.

The riverbank is much too densely overgrown for me to carry on hiking along it. I know stingrays rest in the riverbanks, so I walk carefully. Progress is so slow that I decide to swim in the middle of the river instead—stingrays won't venture into the deep water. I have to look out for piranhas, but I've learned that fish are dangerous only in standing water. I also expect to encounter caimans, alligator-like reptiles, but they generally don't attack people.

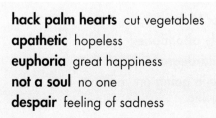

▼ hoatzin

hack palm hearts cut vegetables
apathetic hopeless
euphoria great happiness
not a soul no one
despair feeling of sadness

▶ **Before You Continue**

1. **Make Connections** How is the author's attitude different from Brian's attitude in "Hatchet?" How does reading Brian's story help you understand this text?

2. **Clarify** Use context clues to figure out the meaning of the phrase *new impetus*.

Each night when the sun sets, I search for a reasonably safe spot on the bank where I can try to sleep. Mosquitoes and small flies called midges buzz around my head and try to crawl into my ears and nose. Even worse are the nights when it rains. Ice-cold drops pelt me, soaking my thin summer dress. The wind makes me **shiver to the core**. On those bleak nights, as I cower under a tree or in a bush, I feel **utterly abandoned**.

By day, I go on swimming, but I'm getting weaker. I drink a lot of river water, which fills my stomach, but I know I should eat something.

One morning, I feel a sharp pain in my upper back. When I touch it, my hand comes away bloody. The sun has burned my skin as I swim. I will learn later that I have **second-degree** burns.

As the days wear on, my eyes and ears fool me. Often I'm convinced I see the roof of a house on the riverbank or hear chickens clucking. I am so horribly tired.

I fantasize about food, from elaborate feasts to simple meals. Each morning it gets harder to stand up and get into the cold water. Is there any **sense in going on**? Yes, I tell myself. I have to keep going.

I spend the tenth day drifting in the water. I'm constantly bumping into logs, and it requires a great deal of strength to climb over them and not break any bones

Amazon River

shiver to the core very cold
utterly abandoned completely alone
second-degree very serious
sense in going on reason to keep going

in these collisions. In the evening, I find a gravel bank that looks like a good place to sleep. I doze off for a few minutes. When I wake up, I see something that doesn't belong here: a boat. I rub my eyes, look three times, and it's still there. A boat!

I swim over and touch it. Only then can I really believe it. I notice a **beaten trail** leading up the bank from the river. I'm sure I'll find people there, but I'm so weak that it takes me hours to make it up the hill.

When I get to the top, I see a small shelter, but no people. A path leads from the shack into the forest. I'm certain that the owner of the boat will emerge at any moment, but no one comes. It gets dark, and I spend the night there.

The next morning, I wake and still no one has **shown up**. It begins to rain, and I crawl into the shelter and wrap a **tarp** around my shoulders.

The rain stops in the afternoon. I no longer have the strength to struggle to my feet. I tell myself that I'll rest at the hut one more day, then keep moving.

At twilight I hear voices. I'm imagining them, I think. But the voices get closer. When three men come out of the forest and see me, they stop in shock.

"I'm a girl who was in the LANSA crash," I say in Spanish. "My name is Juliane." ❖

beaten trail path that has been used often
shown up come; appeared
tarp plastic sheet

▶ **Before You Continue**

1. **Draw Conclusions** What will happen to Diller now that she has found people? How do you know?
2. **Use Text Evidence** What examples and evidence from the story illustrate what Diller is like?

Respond and Extend

Compare Choices

The main characters in the selections "Hatchet" and
"Survival Stories: The Girl Who Fell from the Sky" both
face many obstacles. Use a comparison chart to compare how the characters
respond to their situations. Then use the information to draw a conclusion about the
choices the characters make in order to survive.

Comparison Chart

	"Hatchet"	**"Survival Stories: The Girl Who Fell from the Sky"**
Person / Character	Brian Robeson	Juliane Koepcke Diller
Problem		
Goal or Motive		
Choices Made to Achieve Goal	1. 2. 3.	1. 2. 3.

Talk Together

What qualities do Juliane and Brian share that help them in a survival situation?
How do these qualities affect the choices they make? Use **Key Words** and cite
text evidence to talk with a partner about your ideas.

Possessive Adjectives and Pronouns

Use possessives to show ownership. A **possessive adjective** identifies who owns something or has something. A **possessive pronoun** refers to the thing owned and who owns or has it.

Grammar Rules **Possessive Adjectives and Pronouns**	
Use a **possessive adjective** before a **noun**. The possessive adjectives are *my, your, his, her, its, our,* and *their*.	The plane adjusted **its wings**. Passengers were upset when **their bags** fell.
A **possessive pronoun** is used in place of one or more **nouns**. The possessive pronouns are *mine, yours, his, hers, ours* and *theirs*.	Both **Juliane Koepcke Diller** and **Brian Robeson** have adventures. **Theirs** are both tales of bravery. **Hers** is a true story. **His** is fiction.

Read Possessive Adjectives and Pronouns

Writers use possessive adjectives and possessive pronouns to make their writing clearer and easier to understand. Read this passage based on "Hatchet." Identify the possessive adjectives and possessive pronouns.

> Brian Robeson was scared. His plane had crashed. Its pilot was gone. "My parents will begin searching," Brian thought. "But for now, all of the life-saving decisions are mine."

Write Possessive Adjectives and Pronouns

Reread the first two pages of "Survival Stories: The Girl Who Fell From the Sky." Write sentences about what happens to Juliane Koepcke Diller. Be sure to include at least two sentences with possessive adjectives and two with possessive pronouns. Then trade sentences with a partner. Find the possessive adjectives and possessive pronouns in each other's sentences.

Write to Inform

Write an Expository Report

Write an expository report on the topic of animal survival. Then add it to a class magazine about how animals survive.

Study a Model

In an expository report, you present information about a topic. You start by introducing a main idea about the topic. Then you illustrate and elaborate on the topic with supporting details and examples. Read an expository report by Gabriel Ponce.

The first sentence introduces the topic in an interesting way.

Each paragraph includes details and examples that support the main idea.

The conclusion repeats the main idea of the report.

Survival in the Dark
By Gabriel Ponce

Humans need night-vision goggles—or at least flashlights—to see in the dark, but not every creature has trouble at night. Many animals have developed amazing adaptations that allow them to survive in the dark.

Some animals rely on senses other than sight to survive in dark habitats. For example, bats use sounds and their echoes to locate food and sense predators in the dark. This ability is called echolocation, and it allows bats to thrive in caves. Other animals, such as mole rats, are almost blind but use their sharp sense of smell to detect predators in the dark.

Other animals adapt to the dark by emitting their own light. This is called bioluminescence. Fireflies use this ability to communicate. Bioluminescence is also useful for creatures that live deep in the ocean where light from the surface does not reach. Two of these "living lights" are appropriately named the lanternfish and flashlight fish.

From bats to fireflies to fish, nature has created many fascinating ways for animals to thrive and survive in the dark.

The main idea is the most important idea about the topic.

Domain-specific vocabulary helps explain the topic.

Prewrite

1. **Choose a Topic to Write About** Think about the science articles you have read on animal survival. Talk with a partner to choose a topic to write about.

Language Frames

Tell Your Ideas	Respond to Ideas
• One interesting thing about this topic is _____ . • I would like people to know _____ . • Writing about _____ will help me _____ .	• I don't know much about _____ . Can you tell me more? • I'm not sure why you want to write about _____ . Can you clarify? • I don't think I agree with your choice because _____ .

> Use sentences and questions like these to choose a topic.

2. **Gather Information** Use self-stick notes to mark important information in books, or take notes and then underline or highlight ideas. You may also use a computer to record and organize the information you find. Always note the sources where you found the information, such as websites, books, or magazines.

3. **Get Organized** Use a main idea chart to help you organize your ideas.

Main Idea Chart

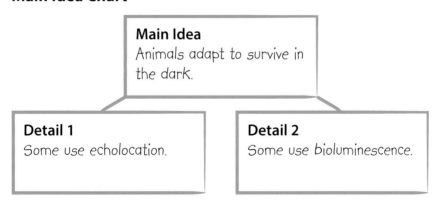

Main Idea
Animals adapt to survive in the dark.

Detail 1
Some use echolocation.

Detail 2
Some use bioluminescence.

Draft

Use the main idea chart and the ideas you collected to write a draft that includes a main idea and supporting details. Be sure to write the ideas in your own words with a style that is appropriate for an expository report.

Revise

1. **Read, Retell, Respond** Read your draft aloud to a partner. Your partner listens and then retells your main points. Then talk about ways to support your main ideas and improve your writing.

Language Frames	
Retell	**Make Suggestions**
• You wrote about _____.	• Your main idea needs to be developed more. Add _____.
• The main idea of your report is _____.	• Could you clarify the detail about _____?
• The important details are _____.	• I like that you included _____. Can you give another example of _____?

2. **Make Changes** Think about your draft and your partner's suggestions. Use revision marks to make your changes.

   • Did you introduce your topic in an interesting way?

   > Humans may need night-vision goggles—or at least flashlights—to see in the dark, but not every creature has trouble at night.
   > ~~In the dark, no one can see.~~

   • Did you include only details related to your main idea? Do you need to delete unnecessary information?

   > Other animals, such as mole rats, are almost blind but use their sharp sense of smell to detect predators in the dark. ~~They are born to serve their queens.~~

Edit and Proofread

Work with a partner to edit and proofread your report. Pay special attention to using pronouns and possessives correctly. Use revision marks to show your changes.

Grammar Tip

Make sure that your pronouns match the words they are replacing by using subject, object, and possessive pronouns correctly.

Present

1. **On Your Own** Make a final copy of your report. Read it to a group of your classmates.

Presentation Tips	
If you are the speaker . . .	**If you are the listener . . .**
Work on pronouncing words correctly. Practice saying any scientific or technical terms.	Listen for the main idea and supporting details.
Adjust your volume, pitch, and tone to keep your report interesting.	Afterward, share your own knowledge and ideas about the topic.

2. **With a Group** Combine your reports into a class magazine. Design a cover and think of a great title. Add graphics to the reports and format them in various ways. Add section heads and use different fonts and colors.

STAYING ALIVE
A Magazine About How Animals Survive

BIG Question

What does it take to survive?

In this unit you found many answers to the **Big Question**. Now use your concept map to discuss it with the class. Think about some things that people and animals need in order to survive.

Concept Map

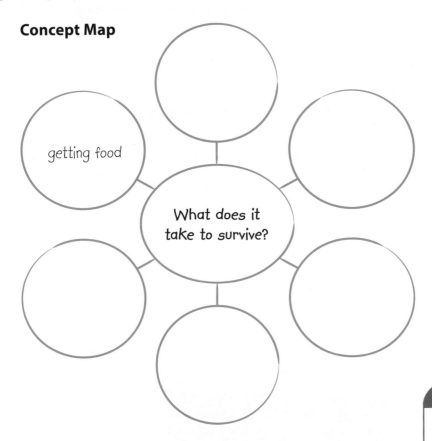

getting food

What does it take to survive?

Performance Task: Explanatory

Consider what you learned from the selections about survival. Write an article for a children's science magazine that explains what living things need in order to survive.

Checklist

Does your article

- ☑ use text evidence from the selections about survival?
- ☑ clearly introduce the topic?
- ☑ include facts, definitions, details, or other information and examples from the sources?
- ☑ include precise language and transition words?

Share Your Ideas

Choose one of these ways to share your ideas about the **Big Question**.

Write It!

Write an Ode

An ode is a short poem written to praise its subject. Write an ode about your favorite animal. Describe how it uses survival skills to get food or to defend itself from predators. Read your ode to the class.

Talk About It!

Do a Mock News Report

Use your knowledge from the unit and pretend that you are a news reporter informing your viewers about a real or imaginary event that includes the topic of survival. Write down some key points that you would like to talk about during your mock news report. Report your story to the class.

Do It!

Make a Presentation

Use the Internet to research a person who had to survive in the wild alone. Use presentation software to describe how the person came to be stranded in the wild and what he or she did to survive. Include pictures, maps, or other visuals in your presentation.

SURVIVAL STORY

Carlos Torres survived at sea for 15 days.

Write It!

Write a Brochure

Imagine that you run a survival camp for people who like the great outdoors. What skills would you teach? What activities would you plan to help campers practice their skills? Use ideas from the selections and from the Internet to plan your camp brochure.

8 WEEK
Survival Camp Training

• build fires
• make shelters
• find food

Unit 3

Digging Up the Past

BIG Question — How can we bring the past to life?

BAHARIYA OASIS, WESTERN DESERT, EGYPT
An archaeologist working on the mummy of a smiling girl
in the Valley of the Golden Mummies

Unit at a Glance
▷ **Language Focus**: Define and Explain, Engage in Discussion
▷ **Reading Strategy**: Ask Questions
▷ **Topic**: Ancient Egypt

Share What You Know

❶ **Think** about objects that can teach us about life in the past.

❷ **Draw** one object and label it.

❸ **Share** your drawing. Explain what it shows about the past.

Language Frames

- _____ means _____.
- For example, _____.
- _____ because _____.

Define and Explain

Look at the photos and listen to the explanation. Listen for definitions of unfamiliar words. Then use **Language Frames** to define or explain something else in the photos.

archaeologist

excavation site

skull

hand tool

hand tool

An Archaeologist at Work 🔊

Archaeologists are scientists who study life in the past. To do this, they often need to excavate historical sites. To excavate means to uncover objects that have been buried in the earth. The objects are buried because layers of debris, or dirt and sand, build up over time. As a result, archaeologists may have to dig deep in order to excavate old buildings, pots, and even bones. They must work slowly and carefully. For example, when excavating delicate objects, they often use hand tools like small shovels and brushes to keep the precious items safe.

Social Studies Vocabulary

🔊 Key Words

Look at the time line and images. Read the captions. Then use **Key Words** and other words to talk about how **archaeological** research, such as digging up objects, can teach us about an ancient **civilization**, or life in a specific country or area.

Key Words
archaeological
artifact
chronological
civilization
dynasty
pharaoh
tomb

Middle Kingdom Dynasties 1975–1640 B.C.E.	New Kingdom Dynasties 1539–1075 B.C.E.	Late Period Dynasties 715–332 B.C.E.

▲ Archaeologists search for clues about how people lived in the past. They may study certain **dynasties**, or periods of time when a specific person or family ruled. Then they can organize the dynasties on a **chronological** time line to show the exact order that the historical periods occurred.

◀ The archaeologist explores a **tomb** where one or more people are buried. This tomb contains the body of someone who died long ago.

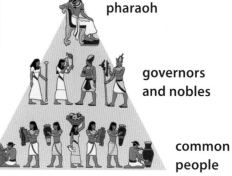

pharaoh

governors and nobles

common people

▲ **Artifacts**, or historical objects like carvings, give the scientists clues that someone important is buried here.

▲ The tomb was built for an ancient **pharaoh**. He was a great leader who ruled as king.

Talk Together

Talk with a partner about how archaeologists uncover information that brings the past to life. Use **Language Frames** from page 142 and **Key Words** to define and explain information that contributes to the topic of archaeology.

Chronological Order

History articles are usually written in **chronological order**, or the exact order in which events happened. But sometimes the author starts with a present-day discovery and then tells what that discovery teaches us about another series of events that occurred in the past. As you read, look for time-order words and phrases to help you determine the sequence of events.

Look Into the Text

In 1827, John Gardner Wilkinson was one of the founders of Egyptology. He designated the tomb KV 5. This meant that it was the fifth tomb beyond the entrance to the King's Valley. Then for more than 150 years, KV 5 was all but forgotten.

In 1989, I was directing a mapping project in the Valley of the Kings. I wanted to relocate KV 5 . . .

"These **time-order words** give clues to the order of events. **Some dates** tell about events that happened more than 150 years ago. **Other dates** tell about a more recent time."

Map and Talk

You can use a double time line to keep track of events that take place in two different time periods.

Double Time Line

Historical Events

1827: Wilkinson named the tomb KV 5.

More Recent Events

1989: The author was looking for KV 5.

Talk Together

Tell a partner about a time you looked at an old family photo or heard a story about something that happened to your family in the past. Write the events you learned about your family on one time line and the present-day events on a second time line.

◉ More Key Words

Use these words to talk about "Valley of the Kings" and "Animals Everlasting."

analytical
adjective

When you study something in an **analytical** way, you break the information into parts so that it is easier to understand. A scientist does an **analytical** study of the liquid by separating it and studying each part.

depict
verb

When you **depict** something, you show it in a picture or with words. The artist's drawing **depicts** the woman.

powerful
adjective

A **powerful** person has the ability to control other people or things. The **powerful** judge makes important decisions in a courtroom.

representation
noun

A **representation** is a picture or other image that stands for a person or thing. This statue is a **representation** of an ancient Egyptian king.

reveal
verb

When you **reveal** something, you show or explain it to others. The magician **reveals** the rabbit that was in his hat.

Talk Together

Work with a partner. Make an Expanded Meaning Map for each **Key Word**.

What the Word Means
an image that stands for a person or thing

Word
representation

Examples
painting, statue, drawing

What It Is Like
looks like the person

145

Learn to Ask Questions

Do you ever wonder about something you have read? Do you ever get confused by a text? Ask yourself a question and then try to find the answer in the text.

How to Ask Questions

1. As you read, pay attention to each question that comes to your mind.

2. Think about where you might find an answer to the question. You can go back and reread the text or keep your question in mind and read on.

3. Think about how the answer helps you understand more about the text.

As I read about _____, I wonder _____.

I can _____.

Now I understand _____.

Here's how one student asked questions and looked for answers in the text.

Look Into the Text

The tomb has turned out to be **the largest ever found** in the Valley of the Kings. **It was a family mausoleum**—the burial place of many of the sons of Ramses II. **It contains at least 110 chambers**, and its artifacts and hieroglyphs promise to change what we know about **Ramses II, one of antiquity's most powerful rulers**.

"As I read **information** about the tomb, I wonder why the tomb is so large."

"I can read on to find more **details** about the tomb."

"Now I understand that the tomb is large because it contains many chambers for the members of a powerful family."

Asking questions helps you learn and clarify new information as you read. It can also help you figure out what is happening in the text and what is important.

Talk Together

Read the news article and sample notes. Use **Language Frames** to ask and answer questions as you read. Talk with a partner about the questions you asked and how you answered them.

News Article

Hunt for a Hidden Tomb

EGYPT, 1989 — Archaeologist Kent Weeks and his team are on the hunt for an Egyptian **tomb** that has been neglected for more than a century. Weeks isn't looking for a major **archaeological** discovery. He is more concerned about plans for construction near the entrance of the Valley of the Kings, the burial site for many of ancient Egypt's most **powerful pharaohs**. Worried that the road construction might damage underground tombs, the team will begin by excavating a tomb known as KV 5, which is considered unimportant by most archaeologists today. ◄

If they do locate KV 5, Weeks and his team are prepared for a great deal of work ahead. Unlike archaeologists who are **depicted** in action movies, these real-life scientists and historians seldom stumble into huge chambers filled with glittering treasures. Instead, their work involves breaking through layers of sand and silt that have washed into the underground tombs over the centuries. In many places, the debris may be like a solid wall of concrete, but there is no way to blast through the barriers without damaging precious, delicate **artifacts**. As a result, it can take days of hard work to **reveal** just a few inches at a time. ◄

If they are lucky, their work will lead to more decades of research and study. Scientists will conduct tests and **analytical** research on any remains found within the tomb. Egyptologists will analyze artwork, such as statues and other **representations** of rulers and gods. By putting the clues together piece by piece, they are often able to reconstruct a **chronological** order of events for important **dynasties** that once ruled over one of the world's most glorious **civilizations**. ◄

As I read about the archaeologists, I wonder why they are looking for such an unimportant tomb.

I can reread the text. It says that Weeks is worried that construction will damage the tomb.

Now I understand that he wants to explore the tomb before it is damaged.

◄ = a good place to stop and ask or answer questions

147

Read a Magazine Article

Genre

Most **magazine articles** are nonfiction. "Valley of the Kings" gives facts and information from the point of view of an archaeologist as he studies ancient Egypt.

Text Features

A **diagram** shows the parts of an object, how a location or building is structured, or how something works. A diagram can include descriptive labels, symbols, or locator numbers that correspond to the information. It can also include a key that tells what the symbols or locator numbers represent.

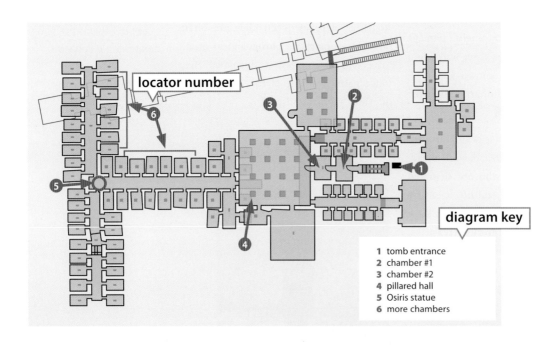

locator number

diagram key

1 tomb entrance
2 chamber #1
3 chamber #2
4 pillared hall
5 Osiris statue
6 more chambers

Valley of the Kings

by Dr. Kent R. Weeks

NATIONAL GEOGRAPHIC EXCLUSIVE

Valley of the Kings, Luxor, Egypt

▶ **Set a Purpose**
Find out how an **archaeological**
team made a remarkable discovery.

███ █ ███   STEPPING INTO THE PAST   ███ █ ███

No one had ventured inside the ancient Egyptian **tomb** since 1825, when a British traveler and **draftsman** named James Burton sketched its first few chambers. The tomb lay somewhere near the entrance to the Valley of the Kings— burial place of New Kingdom **pharaohs** who ruled Egypt at the peak of its military power, between 1539 and 1078 B.C.E.

In 1827, John Gardner Wilkinson was one of the **founders of Egyptology**. He designated the tomb KV 5. This meant that it was the fifth tomb beyond the entrance to the King's Valley. Then for more than 150 years, KV 5 was all but forgotten.

In 1989, I was directing a **mapping project** in the Valley of the Kings. I wanted to relocate KV 5, not because it held treasures—it didn't—but because the roadway at the valley's entrance was being widened. The roadwork seemed likely to damage any tomb in its path. That path, I believed, lay right above KV 5.

The tomb has turned out to be the largest ever found in the Valley of the Kings. It was a family mausoleum—the burial place of many of the sons of Ramses II. It contains at least 110 chambers, and its **artifacts** and **hieroglyphs** promise to change what we know about Ramses II, one of **antiquity's** most **powerful** rulers. During his long reign, ancient Egypt controlled lands from present-day Sudan northeast into Syria. Of all the pharaohs, he was the most prolific builder. To glorify his name, Ramses II erected dozens of imposing temples and monuments along the Nile.

---

draftsman person who makes blueprints and other technical drawings
founders of Egyptology first archaeologists to study ancient Egypt

mapping project team to locate and map **tombs**
hieroglyphs ancient Egyptian writing
antiquity's the ancient past's

RAMSES II FAMILY TREE

Ramses II was a **powerful pharaoh** who had a long, successful rule during Egypt's nineteenth **dynasty**. Egyptologists are still investigating how many children Ramses II had with his wives, but Dr. Kent Weeks estimates that up to 20 of his sons are buried in KV 5. Below is a family tree that includes Ramses II's known children with Queen Isetnofret.

Because archaeologists are still uncovering clues about ancient Egyptian history, many of the dates and details are approximate.

Ramses I ———— Sitre
ruled 1298–1296 B.C.E.

Seti I ———— Tuya
ruled 1290–1279 B.C.E.

Isetnofret ———— **Ramses II**
ruled 1279–1213 B.C.E.

Prince Ramses

Princess Bintanath

Prince/ High-Priest Khaemwaset

Merneptah
ruled 1213–1203 B.C.E.

Princess Isetnofret B

▶ Before You Continue

1. **Cause/Effect** Why did Weeks try to relocate **tomb** KV 5?
2. **Use Text Features** What important information does the family tree show about the **dynasty** of Ramses II?

On a hot Tuesday morning in July 1989, our workmen began digging just east of the roadway. With crude homemade hoes, they scraped away debris. This they carted off in baskets made of old automobile tires. This was standard **archaeological** equipment in Egypt. A week of digging **revealed** traces of a **tomb** entrance. We could see that a narrow **trench** had been cut through the debris clogging the tomb's doorway.

Assistant excavation director Catharine Roehrig, senior workman Muhammad Mahmoud, and I squeezed into the trench. Soon, we were painfully pulling and pushing ourselves over thousands of sharp limestone fragments. To our left and right, the tomb was packed nearly to the ceiling with silt and limestone chips washed in by flash floods.

According to Burton's sketch, the third **chamber** was a **cavernous, pillared hall**. As we crawled along the trench, we could see the broken tops of massive pillars jutting up through the debris. The trench made a sharp turn to the right to avoid a pillar. Then it began weaving between two- and three-ton slabs of limestone that had fallen from the ceiling. No part of the ceiling appeared to have collapsed since Burton's visit in 1825, but the fallen blocks **were unnerving nevertheless**. A headline flashed through my mind: "Egyptologists Flattened as Tomb Collapses. **Pharaoh's** Curse Returns."

After 20 minutes in the stifling heat, we were ready to leave. Soaking wet, sweat streaking my glasses, covered in mud, and with my flashlight fading, I turned to Muhammad. "Do you remember where the entrance is?"

"No."

Catharine wasn't sure either. The hall was so filled with debris that we couldn't see more than a few inches in any direction.

"I think we came in from over there," Muhammad said. He crawled forward, looking for a recognizable pillar or scrape in the debris that would show where we'd been. Shining his flashlight around the chamber, he looked up at the ceiling for a moment. Then he called us over.

trench ditch
chamber room
cavernous, pillared hall large hallway with tall columns
were unnerving nevertheless still worried me

Dr. Kent Weeks (in white hat) and excavation foreman Ahmed Mahmoud Hassan examine a **tomb** that is being cleared in KV 5.

"Look," he said. Directly above him, we could see crude black letters written with the smoke of a candle: BURTON 1825.

After a few more wrong turns, we clambered out of the **tomb**. Catharine scraped mud from her clothes. She wondered aloud about the **tomb's original occupants**. "Remember Elizabeth Thomas? She thought this might be a tomb for children of Ramses II. Thomas didn't have any proof. But she knew more about the Valley of the Kings than any other Egyptologist in this century. Her theory should be checked out."

tomb's original occupants people who were buried there

▶ **Before You Continue**

1. **Ask Questions** Why was Weeks worried while his team explored the tomb? Reread the text to find the answer.

2. **Explain** What evidence did the team find to prove that they had relocated KV 5?

Between 1539 and 1078 B.C.E., almost every pharaoh was buried in the Valley of the Kings.

EXPLORING THE VALLEY

I decided to become an Egyptologist when I was eight, my interest in an ancient **civilization** winning out over dreams of **intergalactic** travel. Although my parents never tried to **dissuade** me from so unlikely a career, one aunt regularly pointed out that an interest in ancient Egypt couldn't possibly lead to a decent job. My friends, **on the other hand**, agreed that cutting open mummies and searching gold-filled **tombs** were worthy goals.

intergalactic space
dissuade stop
on the other hand however

Not long after I **took my Ph.D.** in Egyptology from Yale, the Oriental Institute at the University of Chicago made me director of its field headquarters in Luxor. This is the modern town built atop ancient Thebes. Surrounded by so many **tombs** and temples, I had a wonderful opportunity to delve into the archaeology of the New Kingdom—Egypt's golden imperial age.

The warrior **pharaohs** of the New Kingdom conquered Palestine and Syria with horse-drawn chariots and other advanced military techniques. For three centuries, Egypt was the strongest nation in the world. At Thebes, the pharaohs built larger and grander temples. They wanted to proclaim the might and wealth that made their religious capital "the queen of cities . . . greater than any other city." The city proper stood on the east bank of the Nile. The **necropolis**, with its royal temples and rock-cut tombs, lay on the west.

Now, seated on a rock outcropping with my back to the Valley of the Kings, I peer down on a series of stony hills. They are pockmarked with the entrances to hundreds, perhaps thousands, of private tombs from the New Kingdom. Most have been **plundered** but not excavated.

At first glance, the Valley of the Kings seems little different from hundreds of other valleys at the desert's edge. Shaped like a human hand with fingers splayed, the Valley of the Kings covers only about seven acres—smaller than nearby valleys. Towering over it is el-Qurn, a 1,500-foot peak shaped like a pyramid. Some Egyptologists believe that this natural symbol of the sun god Re led to the selection of the Valley of the Kings as the site of royal tombs. Another reason was security. There's only one narrow **gorge** leading into the valley.

Centuries ago, Roman travelers scratched their names on tomb walls. Ancient robbers **despoiled** most of the royal mummies. Then they carted away the treasures buried with the mummies so that the deceased could live as they had on Earth—furniture, papyrus scrolls, amulets, jewelry, ritual objects, statues. Napoleon Bonaparte brought a team of scholars to record Egyptian antiquities when his army invaded in 1798. Adventurers and archaeologists in the 19th and 20th centuries entered tomb after tomb. Now our team was ready to uncover what time, weather, and careless humans had left behind.

took my Ph.D. got my top academic degree
necropolis ancient cemetery
plundered robbed
gorge passage of land
despoiled stole or destroyed

▶ **Before You Continue**

1. **Chronological Order** What important events happened to KV 5 before Weeks began his work in 1989?

2. **Use Text Evidence** Why was the Valley of the Kings a good location for the **tombs** of Egyptian **pharaohs**?

First, University of Michigan Egyptology student Marjorie Aronow, Ahmed Mahmoud, and I cleared the doorway in the rear wall of the pillared hall. Then we began digging in the chamber beyond, which we assumed would be small. I struggled through the narrow crawl space into the chamber.

"Look," Ahmed said. He was pointing to a gap in the wall of debris that lay ahead.

I shone my flashlight into the gap. There was nothing but blackness. Strange, I thought. The light should reflect off a wall. Crawling forward, we found the **corridor**. It was about nine feet wide and continued a hundred feet into the hillside. There was one door on the left, another on the right, then two more, then four. We counted doors as we crawled forward: 10, 12, 16, 18. Other **tomb** corridors in the Valley of the Kings have at most one or two doorways cut into their walls. I had never seen a corridor like this one in any Egyptian tomb.

Ahmed pointed his flashlight down the corridor. "What's that?" he asked suddenly.

Marjorie gasped. As we turned our flashlights that way, a human form took shape. Ahmed began whispering a prayer from the Koran.

The figure stood ghostlike at the end of the corridor. As we **inched** closer, the form became clearer. It was a five-foot carving. Even though the face was missing, we recognized it as the god of the afterlife, Osiris.

It was a strange feeling. There we sat, 200 feet underground in utter silence, our light focused on an image of the god of the afterlife. For an instant, it was 1275 B.C.E again, and this was ancient Thebes. I could imagine priests chanting prayers and shaking tambourines. I could feel the floor tremble as great **sarcophagi** were dragged down the corridor. I could smell incense and feel priestly robes brush my arm as the **funeral procession** moved slowly past.

corridor passageway
inched moved slowly
sarcophagi decorated coffins
funeral procession line of people going to
     the burial

Weeks's team discovered this statue of Osiris at the end of a corridor in KV 5. Osiris was the Egyptian god of the afterlife, the underworld, and the dead.

▶ **Before You Continue**

1. **Visualize** Which details from Weeks's description best help you imagine an Egyptian funeral procession?

2. **Make Inferences** How does Weeks feel about the discoveries that were **revealed** in KV 5? Support your inference with details.

Finally I aimed my **beam** at the doorways to the left and right of the statue. More surprises. These doors didn't lead to small side chambers, as the other doorways in the corridor did. Instead, they led into yet other corridors that extended even deeper into the bedrock. And there were yet more doorways cut into *their* walls.

"I can't believe it," Marjorie kept repeating.

Suddenly KV 5 had gone from a small, unimportant **tomb** to . . . to what? We crawled back down the corridor, re-counting the doors.

Dr. Kent Weeks and his wife Susan examine a hundred-foot hallway in KV 5 which is lined with doors and chambers. At the end of the corridor is the statue of Osiris.

beam flashlight

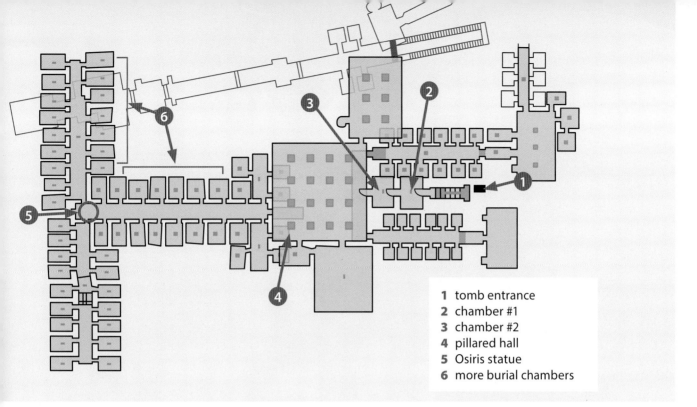

▲ A diagram of KV 5 based on decades of work from Weeks's Theban Mapping Project

1 tomb entrance
2 chamber #1
3 chamber #2
4 pillared hall
5 Osiris statue
6 more burial chambers

"There have to be over 65 chambers in the **tomb**," I said. I was **underestimating**, as we later discovered. No tomb in the Valley of the Kings has more than 30 chambers. Most have only six or eight.

And there was something else. **Inscriptions** in Chambers 1 and 2 indicated that KV 5 was the burial place of several sons of Ramses II. Of the 30-plus sons, we knew that Merneptah was buried in his own tomb in the Valley of the Kings. Two others may also have had separate tombs. Could the rest be here in KV 5? Could the corridors slope downward to a lower level of rooms? Or might other corridors descend to a cluster of burial chambers?

Marjorie, Muhammad, and I were the first people in **millennia** to see these corridors, to touch these carvings, to breathe this stale air. What a humbling experience to sit where Ramses II had come on sad occasions to bury his sons. None of us said a word.

Twenty minutes later, we crawled out of the tomb. We were sweating and filthy and smiling. As the **magnitude** of our discovery began to sink in, I thought to myself: "I know how we're going to be spending the next 20 years."

underestimating guessing too low
Inscriptions Carvings
millennia thousands of years
magnitude size and importance

▶ Before You Continue

1. **Details** What evidence supports the idea that KV 5 was an important discovery for the archaeologists?

2. **Use Text Features** How does the diagram above give information that supports the author's text description of KV 5?

The burial chambers in KV 5 include human remains and fragments of canopic jars, which once held the organs of the deceased. This complete set was used for a young **pharaoh** named King Tutankhamun whose **tomb** was discovered in KV 62.

STUDYING THE PHARAOHS

Outliving at least 12 of his sons, Ramses II ruled for an impressive 66 years. During his long reign, Ramses II expanded and secured Egypt's borders. He built grandiose temples and colossal statues of himself up and down the Nile Valley.

Ramses II died in August 1213 B.C.E., when he was about 90 years old. His **tomb** lies less than 200 feet from KV 5. It remains one of the great unknowns in the Valley of the Kings. Though the entrance corridor is accessible, thick layers of flood debris still fill most of the tomb. That makes our knowledge of its art and architecture **sketchy**. At some places, the debris was so deep, we were often unsure whether we were walking down sloping corridors or silt-covered stairways.

Ramses II was worshiped as a **deity** in his own time. Since he was a living god, his sons attended to many of his **secular** duties. They worked in their father's place, settling legal **disputes** and **conducting foreign relations**. They also oversaw Egypt's

sketchy incomplete
deity god
secular non-religious
disputes disagreements

conducting foreign relations communicating with rulers or governments from other nations

agriculture, irrigation, and economy. This may explain why a **tomb** as unusual as KV 5 came into existence. His sons held positions of greater responsibility than crown princes had in the past. So, when they died before he did, each was given a tomb more elaborate than that of an ordinary prince. Each may have had not only a burial chamber but also several beautifully decorated rooms filled with offerings and funerary goods.

This past year, we unearthed an adult male skeleton from a pit in Chamber 2. Was he a son of Ramses II? Toward the center of the pit, we uncovered the mummified leg of a young cow. This must have been one of the food offerings that had been brought to the tomb to **sustain the deceased** in the afterlife. Another day, we found three human skulls.

Excavating the skeleton proved extremely difficult. The bones were soft. The fragments were embedded in mud and limestone chips. We had to work with dental picks and artists' brushes to loosen the debris and gently brush it away. Some bones were in bad shape. We had to apply a thin solution of **adhesive** every few minutes to keep them from disintegrating.

I squatted in a space only 30 inches wide, braced against the wall with one hand to keep from falling over while I cleaned the skeleton with the other. It often took 10 or 15 minutes to clean and **stabilize** a single square inch. Every half hour, one of the workmen had to help me out of the pit. I needed time to **hobble about** and restore my blocked circulation.

Most Egyptian **pharaohs** were mummified and then buried in decorated coffins called sarcophagi. Many of these precious **artifacts** were stolen or destroyed in KV 5.

sustain the deceased feed the dead
adhesive glue
stabilize prepare
hobble about stretch and move

▶ **Before You Continue**

1. **Use Text Evidence** What evidence supports the idea that the sons of Ramses II were well-respected?

2. **Explain** What are some of the challenges that archaeologists face when excavating **tombs** like KV 5?

Dr. Kent Weeks and his wife Susan stand by the statue of Osiris in KV 5. Their team analyzes decorations and pieces together fragments to learn about the lives and beliefs of ancient Egyptians.

To find out if the skulls and skeletons belong to Ramses's sons, we'll need to run **DNA analyses**. X-rays and other tests will tell us their age at death, cause of death, **ailments**, and injuries. These are the parts of life no hieroglyphic texts ever discuss.

We have collected so much material from KV 5 that it will take us years to analyze it all. There are fragments of **plaster reliefs** to compare with decorations in other **tombs**. There is pottery to reconstruct and date. We also have bones to identify and test. As a general rule, one day's work in the field **generates** three or four days' work in the laboratory, library, computer room, and office.

Just before shutting down our work for the season, we removed the three skulls from the pit. We left the skeleton in place. At some point we'll have him x-rayed. But for now, as our excavation foreman said, "We can let him sleep." ❖

DNA analyses analytical tests on cells in the bones
ailments illnesses
plaster reliefs carvings and statues
generates leads to

THE WORK CONTINUES

The temples, monuments, and **tombs** of ancient Egypt have been uncovered and studied for centuries. But when Dr. Kent Weeks first went to Egypt in 1978, he had difficulty finding many of the **archaeological** sites he had traveled so far to see.

"The need for a **comprehensive** map of Thebes struck me as urgent," Weeks said. "I decided to do something about it."

Weeks created a specialized team whose goal was to record significant archaeological, geographic, and **ethnographic** features in the ancient Egyptian capital of Thebes. The team focused on the Valley of the Kings, where it rediscovered the forgotten entrance to KV 5 in 1989.

Two and a half decades later, Weeks's organization, now known as the Theban Mapping Project (TMP), still has a great deal of work to do. Centuries of **looters**, careless researchers, and an increase in tourism have threatened precious Egyptian sites. As a result, the team has expanded its work to several different areas:

- The TMP continues to excavate KV 5. It is producing 3-D models of the tombs.
- In 2000, it published the *Atlas of the Valley of the Kings*. This is updated annually on the TMP website as new discoveries are made.
- In 2004, it created a management plan that would preserve archaeological sites in the Valley of the Kings.
- In 2011, the TMP opened a public library with texts in Arabic and English. Its goal is to educate researchers, government planners, and even children about Egypt's rich history.

By continuing this work, Weeks and the TMP hope to protect and preserve the wonders of ancient Egypt for generations to come.

comprehensive full and complete
ethnographic cultural
looters people stealing treasures

▶ **Before You Continue**

1. **Ask Questions** What work still needs to be done in KV 5? Look for evidence in the text to find an answer.
2. **Summarize** In your own words, describe the goals of the Theban Mapping Project.

Think and Respond

Key Words

analytical	dynasty
archaeological	pharaoh
artifact	powerful
chronological	representation
civilization	reveal
depict	tomb

Talk About It

1. How do text features like diagrams and photos present information in different ways? How does a specific example from the magazine article add to your understanding of the topic?

2. Imagine that you are Dr. Kent Weeks. Explain the significance of your team's rediscovery of **tomb** KV 5 based on evidence from the text.

3. Why is understanding **chronological** order important when reading this magazine article? Use examples from the text to support your answer.

4. What questions do you still have about the **archaeological** process used by Weeks and his team? How can you find answers to your questions?

5. Analyze how Weeks used details from the **artifacts** he found to make inferences about Ramses II and his sons.

6. What can you generalize about Egyptian burial practices based on what you read about KV 5? Use text evidence to support your generalization.

Write About It

When he was young, Dr. Weeks's aunt discouraged him from becoming an archaeologist. Write an email from Dr. Weeks to his aunt to explain why he became an Egyptologist and why his work is important. Use at least three **Key Words**.

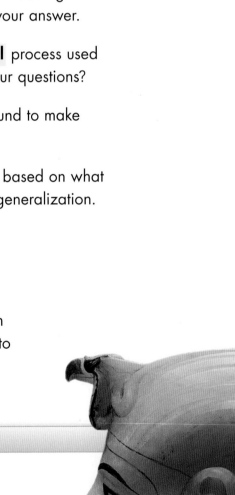

● ○ ○ ✉   My Amazing Job

Dear Aunt Janice,

Do you remember a conversation we had when I was eight? You thought it was a horrible idea for me to dream of an **archaeological** career. I wanted to write to you now to tell you what I have learned about this amazing job.

Chronological Order

Use the double time line to record events from "Valley of the Kings." In your own words, write about the events that happened to different archaeologists and the events that occurred in ancient Egypt.

Double Time Line

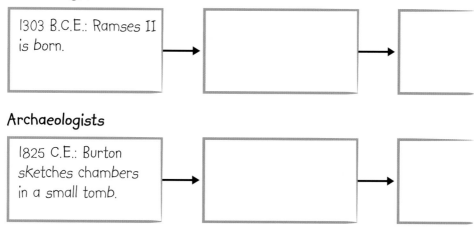

Ancient Egyptians

1303 B.C.E.: Ramses II is born.

Archaeologists

1825 C.E.: Burton sketches chambers in a small tomb.

Summarize the important events from the first time line to a partner. Tell the events in **chronological** order, and explain how the events are related. Your partner summarizes events from the second chain. Use **Key Words**.

Fluency

Practice reading with phrasing. Rate your reading.

Talk Together

Which specific details from "Valley of the Kings" brought the ancient past to life for you? Discuss your ideas with a partner. Use **Key Words** and text evidence to share your ideas.

Word Work

Suffixes and Base Words

A **base word** is a complete word that makes sense by itself. You can add a **suffix** to the end of a base word to change its meaning or how it is used in a sentence. Sometimes, the spelling of the base word changes when you add a suffix.

EXAMPLES

The suffix *-ful* means "full of."

power + -ful = powerful

The suffix *-ion* means "the action of."

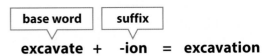

excavate + -ion = excavation

Base Word	Suffix	New Word	Meaning
govern	-or	governor	a person who governs
ornament	-al	ornamental	having the characteristics of an ornament
examine	-ation	examination	the result of examining

The chart above shows some other common suffixes. The suffix *-al* means "having the characteristics of." What do you think *archaeological* and *chronological* mean?

Try It

Read the sentences. Then answer the questions. Use the chart to help you.

> The <u>excavator</u> carefully uncovered several clay pots. The pots were covered with paintings, carvings, and other <u>representations</u> of pharaohs.

1. **Look at the suffix *-or*. What is the best meaning for the word <u>excavator</u>?**

   A   an area where people excavate

   B   an object that has been excavated

   C   a room to store excavated items

   D   a person who excavates

2. **Look at the suffix *-ation*. What is the best meaning for the word <u>representations</u>?**

   A   pots that represent

   B   images that represent

   C   areas that represent

   D   people who represent

Making Connections You read about how an Egyptologist **revealed** facts about a **powerful** **pharaoh**. Now read about how another archaeologist reveals facts about everyday people in ancient Egypt.

Genre A **magazine article** is usually nonfiction text that gives facts and information about a topic.

ANIMALS EVERLASTING

by A. R. Williams

For many decades, archaeologists and treasure seekers led expeditions through the Egyptian desert. Their **quest** was to find royal **tombs** and splendid gold and painted masks and coffins. These would be sent to adorn the estates and museums of Europe and America. Lying among the ancient **artifacts** lay many thousands of mummified animals that turned up at **sacred** sites throughout Egypt. To those early explorers, the carefully preserved remains were just things to be cleared away to get at the good stuff. Few people studied them, and their importance was generally unrecognized.

◀ **cat mummy from Abydos, Egypt**

quest goal
sacred religious

▶ **Before You Continue**

1. **Author's Viewpoint** What evidence from the text shows the author's opinion about the early treasure seekers?

2. **Ask Questions** Where were the animal mummies found? Reread or read on to find the answer.

167

▲ Ikram studies the mummy of an ibis—a bird once worshipped in ancient Egypt.

In the past century, archaeology has become less of a trophy hunt and more of a science. Excavators now realize that much of their sites' wealth lies in the multitude of details about ordinary folks. Archaeologists want to know what they did, what they thought, how they prayed. Animal mummies are a big part of that **pay dirt**.

"They're really **manifestations of** daily life," says Egyptologist Salima Ikram. "Pets, food, death, religion. They cover everything the Egyptians were concerned with." Ikram specializes in zooarchaeology—the study of ancient animal remains. She has helped launch a new line of research into cats and other creatures that were preserved with great skill and care. As a professor at the American University in Cairo, she adopted the Egyptian Museum's **languishing** collection of animal mummies as a research project. She spent time taking precise measurements, peering beneath linen bandages with x-rays, and **cataloging** her findings. Then she created a gallery for the collection. The result was a bridge between people today and those of long ago. "You look at these animals, and suddenly you say, Oh, King So-and-So had

pay dirt reward they want
manifestations of information about
languishing forgotten; ignored
cataloging recording

a pet. I have a pet. And instead of being at a distance of 5,000-plus years, the ancient Egyptians become people."

Today the animal mummies are one of the most popular exhibits in the whole treasure-filled museum. Visitors of all ages, Egyptians and foreigners, press in shoulder to shoulder to get a look. Behind glass panels lie cats wrapped in strips of linen that form diamonds, stripes, squares, and crisscrosses. Shrews in boxes of carved limestone. Rams covered with gilded and beaded casings. A gazelle wrapped in a tattered mat of papyrus, so thoroughly flattened by mummification that Ikram named it Roadkill. A 17-foot, knobby-backed crocodile, buried with baby croc mummies in its mouth. Ibises in bundles with intricate **appliqués**. Hawks. Fish. Even tiny scarab beetles and the dung balls they ate.

Some animal mummies were preserved so that the deceased would have companionship in eternity. Ancient Egyptians who could afford it prepared their **tombs** lavishly. They hoped that their assembled personal items would magically be available to them after death. Beginning in about 2950 B.C.E., kings of the 1st **dynasty** were buried at Abydos with dogs, lions, and donkeys. More than 2,500 years later, during the 30th dynasty, a commoner at Abydos named Hapi-men was laid to rest with his small dog curled at his feet.

Other mummies were **provisions** for the dead. The best cuts of beef, succulent ducks, geese, and pigeons were salted, dried, and wrapped in linen. "Victual mummies" is what Ikram calls this gourmet jerky for the **hereafter**. "Whether or not you got it regularly in life didn't matter because you got it for eternity."

And some animals were mummified because they were sacred animals. They were worshipped at their own **cult** centers—bulls at Armant and Heliopolis, fish at Esna, rams at Elephantine Island, crocodiles at Kom Ombo. Ikram believes the idea of such divine creatures was born at the dawn of Egyptian **civilization**. It was a time when heavier rainfall than today made the land green and bountiful. Surrounded by animals, people began to connect them with specific gods according to their habits.

Take crocodiles, symbols of Sobek, a water god. Captive crocodiles led an **indulged** life and were buried with due ceremony after death.

appliqués decorations
provisions food and supplies
hereafter afterlife
cult religious
indulged easy; protected

▶ **Before You Continue**
1. **Explain** Why does Ikram believe it is important to study animal mummies?
2. **Draw Conclusions** What do animal mummies show about how ancient Egyptians viewed the afterlife?

The most numerous mummies, buried by the millions as at the site of Istabl Antar, were votive objects. These were offered up during yearly festivals at the temples of animal cults. Like county fairs, these great gatherings enlivened religious centers up and down the Nile. **Pilgrims** arrived by the hundreds of thousands and set up camp. Music and dancing filled the **processional route**. Merchants sold food, drink, and souvenirs. Priests became salesmen, offering simply wrapped mummies. They also provided more elaborate ones for people who could spend more—or thought they should. With incense swirling all around, the faithful ended their journey by delivering their chosen mummy to the temple with a prayer.

Some places were associated with just one god and its symbolic animal. But old, **venerated** sites, such as Abydos, have yielded whole **menageries** of votive mummies, each species a link to a

crocodile mummy from the 1st century B.C.E.

Pilgrims Travelers
processional route road to the temple
venerated important and respected
menageries collections

particular god. At Abydos, the burial ground of Egypt's first rulers, excavations have uncovered ibis mummies. These likely represented Thoth, the god of wisdom and writing. Falcons probably evoked the sky-god Horus, protector of the living king. And dogs had ties to the jackal-headed Anubis, the guardian of the dead. By donating one of these mummies to the temple, a pilgrim could win favor with its god. "The creature was always whispering in the god's ear. It said, 'Here he is, here comes your **devotee**, be nice,'" explains Ikram.

Part of Ikram's work is to find out how the ancient **embalmers** worked—a subject on which the ancient texts are silent or **ambiguous**. Therefore, she conducts experiments in mummification. Using rabbits purchased from local butchers, she studies different processes and materials that ancient embalmers may have used.

Like the animals mummified more than 3,000 years ago, Ikram's test subjects went to a happy afterlife. Once the lab work was done, she and her students followed **protocol** and wrapped each body in bandages printed with magical spells. Reciting prayers and burning incense, they laid the mummies to rest in a classroom cabinet, where they **draw** visitors— including me. As an offering, I sketch plump carrots and symbols to multiply the bunch by a thousand. Ikram assures me that the pictures have instantly become real in the hereafter, and her rabbits are twitching their noses with joy. ❖

devotee faithful follower

embalmers people who prepared the dead for burial

ambiguous unclear

protocol the proper steps

draw attract

▶ **Before You Continue**

1. **Summarize** Why did ancient Egyptians create animal mummies? Cite specific examples from the text.

2. **Make Inferences** How do Ikram and her students treat their mummy experiments? Why do they do this?

ANIMAL MUMMIES

This map shows various sites in Egypt where animal mummies have been discovered.

Mediterranean Sea

NILE RIVER DELTA

Sais

Tanis
Avaris
Mendes
Bubastis

Heliopolis
Cairo
Abu Rawash
Giza

Saqqara (a cemetery of Memphis)

Atfih

Abu Sir al Malaq

El Faiyum

E G Y P T

Gulf of Suez

ANIMAL MUMMIES
Species buried in select areas

Site

Cat

Cow/Bull

Crocodile

Dog

Donkey

Elephant

Fish

Gazelle

Horse

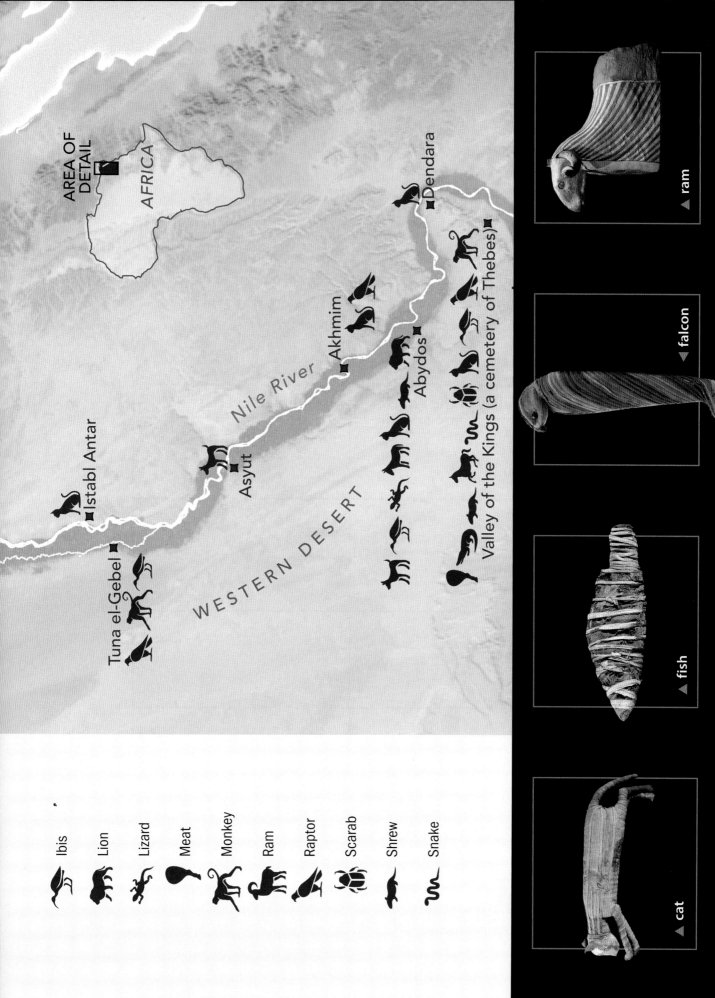

AREA OF
DETAIL

AFRICA

Istabl Antar

Tuna el-Gebel

Nile River

Asyut

WESTERN DESERT

Akhmim

Abydos

Dendara

Valley of the Kings (a cemetery of Thebes)

Ibis

Lion

Lizard

Meat

Monkey

Ram

Raptor

Scarab

Shrew

Snake

▲ ram

▲ falcon

▲ fish

▲ cat

Key Words

analytical	dynasty
archaeological	pharaoh
artifact	powerful
chronological	representation
civilization	reveal
depict	tomb

Compare Information

Both "Valley of the Kings" and "Animals Everlasting" describe **archaeological** discoveries from ancient Egypt. Work with a partner to compare the way information is presented in the two selections. Record examples in the comparison chart and then discuss how reading both selections helped you synthesize, or put together, information about the ancient **civilization** of Egypt.

Comparison Chart

	"Valley of the Kings"	**"Animals Everlasting"**
Topic		An Egyptologist studies animal mummies.
Text	details about the structure, art, remains, and chambers in the tomb	
Main Ideas		
Text Features		

Talk Together

How do Weeks's and Ikram's discoveries add to our knowledge of the ancient past? How does that information help bring the past to life? Use **Key Words** and cite evidence from the text to talk about your ideas.

Progressive Tenses

The **progressive tense** tells about an action that occurs over a period of time. The main verb always ends in **–ing**.

Grammar Rules Progressive Tenses

• A **present progressive verb** tells about an action as it is happening. It uses the auxiliary verb **am**, **is**, or **are**.	Dr. Weeks **is working** in KV 5.
• A **past progressive verb** tells about an action that was happening over a period of time in the past. It uses the auxiliary verb **was** or **were**.	He **was searching** for clues about Ramses II for many years.
• A **future progressive verb** tells about an action that will be happening over a period of time in the future. It uses the auxiliary verbs **will be**.	Future archaeologists **will be using** new analytical tools for many years.

Read Progressive Tenses

Some writers use progressive tenses to clarify whether actions happen in the past, present, or future. Read this passage based on "Valley of the Kings." How do auxiliary verbs show when each action takes place?

For months in 1989, Dr. Kent Weeks and his team were investigating a small tomb in the Valley of the Kings. Their work revealed a huge tomb complex. Today, the archaeologists are excavating dozens of chambers in the tomb. Their discoveries are changing what we know about life in ancient Egypt. They will be studying these treasures for decades to come.

Write Progressive Tenses

Reread page 150 of "Valley of the Kings," and write a short paragraph to summarize the information. Include at least one sentence for each progressive tense. Then compare your sentences with a partner's.

Language Focus

Engage in Discussion

Listen to Oscar and Emre's discussion with their teacher. Then use **Language Frames** to engage in a discussion about historical stories.

Language Frames

- I agree with _____ because _____ .
- What can you learn about _____ from _____ ?
- I think you said _____ . Is that right?
- I'd like to add on. I think _____ .

Stories of the Past

Oscar: My family went to the museum on Saturday. We've been reading about ancient Egypt in class, but after seeing the exhibit there, I've decided that museums are the best way to learn about history.

Emre: I agree with Oscar about museums because I saw the same exhibit last summer. Watching documentaries and reading nonfiction books are helpful, but there's something really fascinating about seeing an actual mummy.

Teacher: I understand what you mean. It's different seeing the real thing. If you prefer seeing real artifacts, what is your opinion about historical fiction? What can you learn about an historical time or place from reading a made-up story?

Emre: I still like reading novels about the past. Even if the characters and events aren't real, the stories make me care about the people who lived in those times.

Teacher: Oscar, I think you said that you learn the most at museums. Is that right?

Oscar: That's right, but I understand Emre's viewpoint about fiction, too. I'd like to add on to that idea. I think that historical fiction is a great way to find out whether you're interested in a topic. Then you can look for other ways to learn about the facts.

Key Words

Key Words
chamber
command
hieroglyphics
peer
plunder
procession

🔊 Key Words

Study the illustration and descriptions. Use **Key Words** and other words to discuss what we learn when we **peer** into ancient tombs.

Death in Ancient Egypt

1 When an important person died in ancient Egypt, people walked together in a funeral **procession** that followed the body as it was carried to the tomb.

2 The dead were buried with food and belongings they would need in the afterlife.

3 Wealthy Egyptians **commanded**, or ordered, that treasures be buried with them. Over the years, robbers **plundered**, or stole, many precious objects.

4 An Egyptian tomb had **chambers**, or special rooms, that were often decorated.

5 **Hieroglyphics**, a form of symbol writing, covered the walls with messages.

Talk Together

How does studying Egyptian tombs bring the past to life? Use **Language Frames** from page 176 and **Key Words** to discuss this question with a group.

Plot

A **plot** is the series of events that happens in a story. It usually begins when a main character encounters a conflict, or problem. Throughout the story, the character responds to major plot events, including the turning point, or climax, of the story. All of the events lead to the final resolution at the end of the story.

My father loves the brushes I make, but he doesn't know I pay special attention when I make them because I like to practice writing hieroglyphics when no one is watching. I will be a craftsman, because that is my father's trade and that is the tradition, but **I wish I could be a scribe and get all the knowledge privileged kids have access to**.

"The **conflict** occurs when the narrator expresses a wish to become a scribe rather than a craftsman. I can read on to learn about the character's response and the next plot events."

Map and Talk

A plot diagram can help you keep track of story events. Analyzing how characters respond to the conflict, events, turning point, and resolution can help you better understand the story.

Plot Diagram

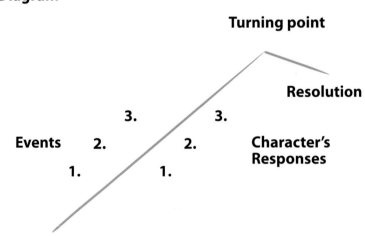

Turning point

Resolution

Events   2.   3.   3.
        1.   2.   **Character's Responses**
                1.

Conflict Ahmes wants to become a scribe.

Talk with a partner about a story you have recently read. Create a plot diagram that identifies how the main character responds to important story events and how the events lead to the resolution of the story.

🔊 More Key Words

Use these words to talk about "Ahmes's Journal" and "The Golden Goblet."

consider
verb

When you **consider** something, you think about it carefully. The boy **considers** which snack to choose.

contribute
verb

To **contribute** means to give something to others. Each student will **contribute** one dollar to help people in need.

impact
noun

An **impact** is the effect one thing has on another. The creative science teacher had a positive **impact** on her students.

perspective
noun

A **perspective** is a point of view. The students discussed their different **perspectives** about the issues.

significant
adjective

Something **significant** is important. Finding King Tut's tomb was a **significant** discovery for archaeologists.

Talk Together

Use a **Key Word** to ask a question. Your partner answers using another **Key Word**, if possible. Use each word twice.

> Will the rain have an impact on the game?

> Yes, rain will have a significant impact on whether we can play today..

Learn to Ask Questions

When you read, you can **ask questions** to help you understand a story and its characters. Sometimes, a question is answered directly in a text. At other times, you have to combine story details with what you already know to infer an answer.

How to Ask Questions

1. As you read, ask yourself questions to understand something confusing, to track what is happening, or to understand the author's viewpoint.

2. Reread the text or read on to find any answers that are right there.

3. If the exact answers are not there, think about the details. Think about what you already know. Put them together to come up with answers for your questions.

As I read, I wonder _____.

I find details about _____ in the text. Now I know _____.

I link _____ and _____ to figure out that _____.

Here's how one student asked a question and found an answer.

Look Into the Text

Father remembered seeing my attempts at writing and **noticing I had an ability for hieroglyphics**. So he took my case to Nebamun's father, who is an **influential person in our community**. My case was **discussed at the school**, and it was decided that my skills should be directed to what I could do best.

"As I read **details** about Ahmes's skills, I wonder how he was able to break tradition and become a scribe."

"I find **details** about Nebamun's father and how he asked the school to accept Ahmes."

Asking yourself questions as you read can help you figure out what is happening and what the author is trying to say.

Language Frames

As I read, I wonder
_____ .

I find details about _____
in the text. Now I Know
_____ .

I link _____ and _____
to figure out that _____ .

Read the historical fiction story and sample notes.
Use **Language Frames** to ask and answer questions
with a partner.

Historical Fiction

A Day *IN THE*
Life of a Scribe

*K*hu worked quickly but carefully as he transcribed the historical text onto a papyrus scroll. The writing teachers **commanded** excellence, and the smallest of mistakes could mean a strike on the back or—worse—starting over. Khu dipped his reed brush into the ink and, with a few swift strokes, was finished. ◀

"Well done, Khu," said a voice at his shoulder. Khu stood at the writing teacher's words. He hadn't heard the teacher approach, and the kind words had a more powerful **impact** on the boy than the punishing sting of a stick.

"I thank you, Teacher," he answered, bowing slightly to hide his pride. To receive such praise was indeed **significant**. ◀

As the teacher departed, Khu surveyed the room. Here and there, younger boys leaned over pottery shards, pieces of wood, or smooth stones, learning to write by copying short sayings and myths. With more than 700 symbols—and many more combinations for layers of meaning—there was much to learn. The older boys, like Khu, used papyrus scrolls, demonstrating their knowledge by copying official documents and histories. ◀

On this night, Khu thought to himself, *Father will take one of these boys as an apprentice.* He **considered** the possibilities. From his **perspective**, Yaferu was the best choice. He was the eldest, and his **hieroglyphics** were sharp and precise. He was quick, honest, and excelled at math. A scribe who could do accounting had much to **contribute** when it was time to tally the harvest or collect taxes.

Khu gathered his tools, packed them into his scribal kit, and headed for the door.

"Khu, wait," Yaferu called out. "I'll come with you. Your father has summoned me to your house, though I know not why."

Khu smiled knowingly as he linked arms with his friend and began to walk home. ◀

As I read, I wonder where Khu is.

I find details about transcribing, texts, writing teachers, and ink in the text. Now I Know that Khu is in a writing school.

I link Khu's actions and what I Know about ancient Egypt to figure out that he is a student learning to be a scribe.

◀ = a good place to stop and ask or answer a question

Read a Diary

Genre

A **diary** is a record of a person's thoughts, feelings, and experiences. "Ahmes's Journal" is a fictional account of a young scribe in ancient Egypt. While the events and most of the characters were created by the author, the setting and descriptions of life in ancient Egypt are based on historical facts.

Setting

The setting of a story is **where** and **when** it takes place. This story is set in ancient Egypt during

the late 18th Dynasty. Look for dates, locations, and other details that can tell you more about the setting.

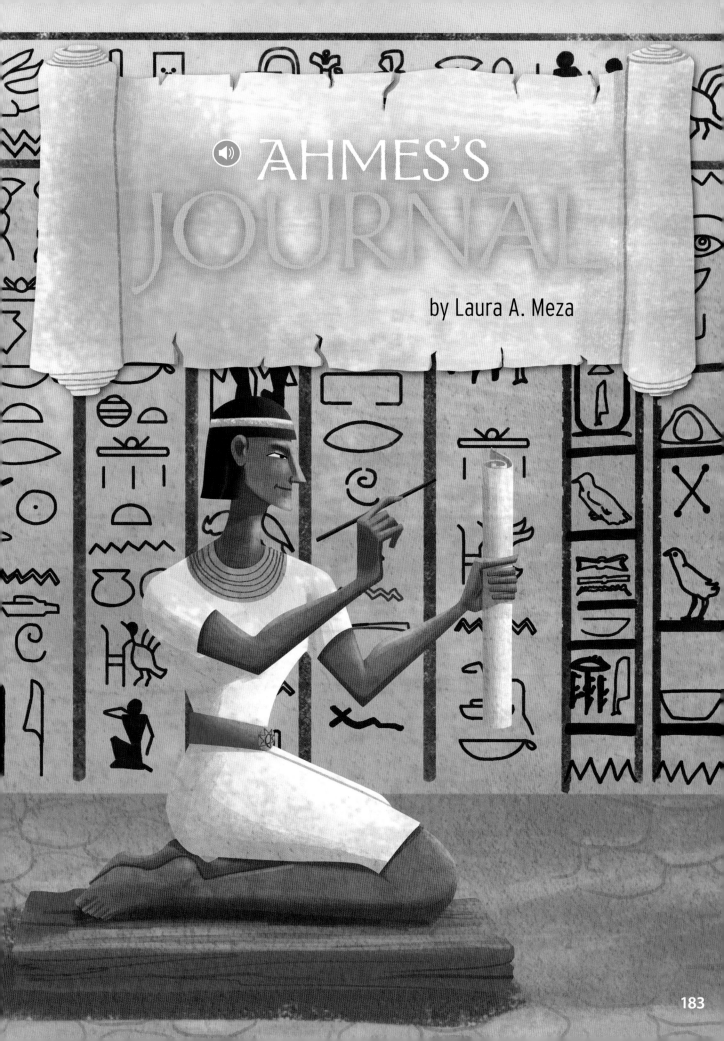

AHMES'S JOURNAL

by Laura A. Meza

▶ **Set a Purpose**
Find out about Ahmes's daily life
growing up in ancient Egypt.

WASE, CAPITAL OF EGYPT

Day one, first month of the planting season

What a heavy day of work at my father's workshop today! Father is **a craftsman**, and in his workshop he makes vases, plates, jewelry, and other objects for everyday use. It is fun to work with him, and I especially love helping him **grind** minerals to create colors for the objects he makes. I grind minerals or burnt organic materials into powder. Then I put them in a vase and add water to make ink.

Along with making ink, I think I am quite good at making the brushes that he uses to paint his craft pieces and that we also sell to people who go to school. The trick is to hammer the end of the **reed** and then rub it continually with a tool, making it as smooth as possible before you use it. My father loves the brushes I make, but he doesn't know I pay special attention when I make them because I like to practice writing **hieroglyphics** when no one is watching. I will be a craftsman, because that is my father's **trade** and that is the tradition, but I wish I could be a **scribe** and get all the knowledge privileged kids have access to. Craftsmen like my father have respect from others and a good life, like ours, but scribes get even more respect because of all the knowledge they can record.

a craftsman an artist who creates things that people use

grind crush

reed tall, slender grass

trade profession

scribe person who keeps written records

Day three, first month of the planting season

Today was a good day. I made a new friend, I think. In the morning, after having a large piece of homemade bread, a few dates, and some milk, I went to the **marshes** with my brother. We started out in the boat just after sunrise, when the light was shining low over the water, making it look like a golden mirror. Most animals were still silent at that time. We were hunting wild birds, hoping to catch something good for dinner. I'm not very good at hunting because I don't have a lot of practice. I'm still learning, and my brother doesn't have the patience to teach me. I do my best and copy what he does, but I don't have his strength yet.

marshes wetlands

When we were about to come back, we noticed another boat with people who were also hunting. The fine linen and leather sandals they were wearing let us know that they were **nobles**. In my family, we wear **coarse** linen and sandals made of reeds, but I like the fabric I wear, as it was my mother who wove it.

I saw Nebamun there. He was the only kid my age in the group, and by observing him and **his party**, I could see this was not the first time he had been hunting. He was skilled beyond belief, throwing sticks at the birds and reaching out from the boat to catch them by the feet. Nebamun almost caught one as I was watching. The bird fought hard and managed to escape in our direction, but it was already badly hurt, so it couldn't fly. Our boat was close, so I jumped off and rushed into the **shallow** water to get the bird. I guess Nebamun thought I was going to run away with it, but I was only trying to help. I handed him the bird, and he smiled at me. I told him my name, and he told me his, and then he said, "Maybe we can see each other later, Ahmes!" I think we might become friends from now on, even if my brother thinks I am being silly.

nobles people with high social status
coarse rough
his party the people he was with
shallow low

Day ten, first month of the planting season

I was not wrong. Nebamun is nice, and we are now friends. I like having a friend my age now that my brother spends more time with Father in the workshop. I will start my **formal training** in making crafts soon. So far, I help with the little things, like making ink and brushes, and then I have time to play with my new friend. We played *senet*, and I got my six cones across the board and back first, so I won the game. I guess Nebamun was not very lucky today. It was late, and we were using an oil lamp to see.

In the other room, Father and Mother were having a serious conversation. Father needs help in his workshop, and my brother tries as much as he can, but he is not very good at doing artwork. Father has three other people to help him, and they all work quite well. My brother is not so good, but he keeps trying. Father is well known and respected in his profession. Noble people come to ask him for special work, but most of what he makes goes to the market, and we sell it there. My mother helps by taking charge of the business part, and she is really smart at this. I worry about my brother. What will happen if he doesn't learn the trade well?

formal training preparation for a career
senet an Egyptian board game

▶ **Before You Continue**

1. **Plot** What is the main conflict, or problem, that Ahmes's family faces?
2. **Setting** What details in the text tell you about life in ancient Egypt?

▶ **Predict**
What changes will happen for
Ahmes's family?

Day twelve, first month of the planting season

Today, Nebamun and I went hunting again. He caught two birds, and I caught one. He enjoys showing off his skill, but he also enjoys my company, I know. He's already teaching me some of the tricks he uses to hunt. We spent the afternoon talking about his school. I had a lot of questions for him, and every detail he told me was fascinating! I started school when I was younger, but I stopped when Father decided I was old enough to train in the family business. I know what happens in a classroom, but listening to Nebamun made me want to go back. He told me how he learns about our history from teachers and how they read and write on clay or on **papyrus**, depending on their skill. Of course, Nebamun uses papyrus, as he is one of the brightest in his class. He told me he's already started copying government documents, and he's focusing on history and math to prepare for his future role as a scribe in charge of grain collection, like his father. He's already using books to prepare for this role! I wish I could go to school like he does, but I'm the son of a craftsman, and I'll learn my father's trade. Nebamun will be a scribe. He'll get to learn more about our writing systems and record important information. That sounds like an interesting job to prepare for.

After discussing our futures, I showed my friend papyrus with samples of my writing. He was surprised when he saw my work with **hieroglyphics**. I normally don't show that to people, but we are friends now, and we share many things. He said my work is even better than his, but I don't believe it. He takes classes and practices more than I do. But I do pay attention to detail, and I like to be very **precise** with the different shapes needed for the many symbols there are.

papyrus thick paper
precise exact

Nebamun asked me whether I wanted to be a scribe, but I explained to him that it wasn't my choice to make. "Father needs me and my brother in the workshop, and trying something different can mean breaking tradition," I said. He then told me a wonderful story. He said that even if girls normally stay at home and help with chores and home businesses, there had been one in his school who practiced with the scribes and learned to read the medical knowledge left by ancestors, for she showed great skill in healing. This girl later became a doctor.

I asked Mother and Father about this story when I got home, and they said it was true. A few women have been educated to become doctors, and many noble women learn to read and write. I couldn't help thinking: If a girl can be allowed to break tradition, maybe there would be a chance for a boy like me to do something different, too. Can it mean that, if I show exceptional skill, Father may let me go to school to become a scribe? But I could never say anything to him about that.

Day fifteen, first month of the planting season

Nebamun and I invent games to play together, and we talk a lot. We play "scribes" with ink and material from Father's workshop. Nebamun says this game helps him study and be better at school. It's fun to draw in **scrolls** and note information we find in the workshop or our homes.

Yesterday, Father came in the room when we were playing. He didn't seem happy with the fact that we were wasting **resources** from the workshop, and he gave me a **stern** look. He said it was nice I was helping my friend study, and then he took a look at the records we made. He said, "Great work, Nebamun. You'll be a great scribe!" Nebamun told him the work he was seeing was mine, not his, and Father just looked at me and left **with no further comment**. I thought he was going to **discipline** me after dinner, because I know papyrus is expensive and shouldn't be used for games, but he didn't say anything. I guess I'll have to ask for permission the next time we use materials from the workshop to play.

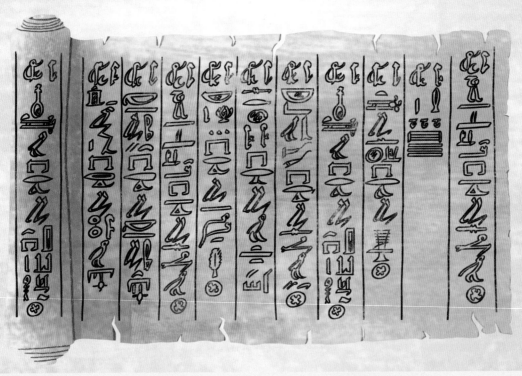

scrolls rolls of paper
resources supplies
stern serious; severe
with no further comment without saying anything else
discipline scold; punish

Day one, second month of the planting season

Today was not a good day for my family. Father knows now that my brother is not good at crafts. His work on jewelry and pottery is slow, and he pays no attention to detail. The other people working at the workshop worry about the quality of the work and think that if my brother continues working there, the reputation of the workshop will be affected.

Father has decided to send my brother away. Father says that if my brother doesn't show talent for the family business, he should go to another village and try his luck on his own. Many families do that. He was hoping my brother could be exceptional as a craftsman so that he could be invited to work in the decoration of temples or tombs, but my brother doesn't have the interest or the skill for that. Mother was not happy about Father's decision to send my brother away. She cried a lot, and the feeling in the house was heavy and sad. In the evening, Mother and Father talked to me to tell me they hoped I could become better at the family's trade and **take over** the workshop one day. Of course, I said I would do my best, and I will. But that means there is no hope for me to become a scribe. I didn't mention it. I don't think I can ever mention it. In the meantime, I continue to write **in private**. I find papyrus and write for myself. My secret passion will not bring my family any happiness for now, so I will be **a dutiful** son and continue to learn the family trade.

take over be in charge of
in private by myself; secretly
a dutiful an obedient

▶ **Before You Continue**

1. **Confirm Predictions / Explain** What happened to Ahmes's brother? Is there evidence to suggest that Ahmes's conflict will be resolved?

2. **Ask Questions** What is Ahmes like? Combine details from the text to find the answer.

191

▶ **Predict**

What will happen to Ahmes now that his brother is gone?

Day ten, second month of the planting season

Since my brother went away, I spend more time with Father, and I have less time to play or go hunting with Nebamun. He is also busy with school, and he gets to go hunting with his father. I am learning to make pots and other pieces to sell at the market. The other workers seem happy with my contributions. They are good at their work and have the patience to teach me what they do and answer my questions. I like my father's workshop and what we do there. We work together on all the pieces.

When you're learning a trade, you must be respectful to those with more experience. They sometimes give direct orders that I have to follow to get the job done. I'm allowed to ask questions and give ideas, but observing and listening to others come first. The work doesn't have anyone's name on it because we all **contribute** to it. My father tells me this also happens in important **commissions**, such as the work for tombs and pyramids. I guess I can be happy in this line of work because it's my heritage. But I still study **hieroglyphics** on my own and talk to Nebamun now and then about his schoolwork, which continues to interest me greatly. Nebamun and I continue to be friends, and my family has been invited to his family's banquet in two days. Mother is very excited, and I am, too. Banquets are always fun, and it's an honor to be invited to one.

commissions orders to create special work

Day thirteen, second month of the planting season

We went to the banquet in honor of Nebamun's father. There were a lot of people there, and we all had fun. The women wore their best linen and jewelry. My mother wore her glass jewelry, which she keeps for occasions like this. Everyone admired the pieces she was wearing, even if they're not as fine or expensive as the gold and silver the other women wore. The air smelled of fine perfume, and beads and other **embellishments** glittered on everyone's clothing. The **atmosphere** was joyful.

embellishments decorations
atmosphere environment

I still can't believe what happened at the banquet. I didn't know my father and Nebamun's father had a surprise for me. When the banquet was almost over, Nebamun's father called my name and asked me, in front of everyone, math problems and questions about our history. I was able to answer all of them, and I didn't **hesitate** when he asked me to read a papyrus with **hieroglyphics** he had written. It wasn't difficult; it was **an account** of activities in his household. I read it **fluently**, and he asked whether I could write something like that. The question made me uncomfortable because I didn't know some things needed to do this hard work. I was silent for a moment, and I looked to the ground. I felt **the weight of the world** on my shoulders. I was wishing my father or mother would say something so that I didn't have to say I couldn't do it. After a moment of silence, with all eyes turned to me, I heard Father's voice telling me, "Ahmes, answer truthfully. The truth is always our friend." So I said, "I could write some of this, but not all. I have many things to learn." I was trying to sound calm and proud, but I could hear my heart pounding and feel the blood rushing to my cheeks. "Very well, then," said Nebamun's father. "You should go to school and study so that you can learn those things, and I hope you can become as good a scribe as my son will be." I could not believe my luck! I was dizzy and silent for a while, but I managed to say, "Thank you, sir. I will be honored." Then I went to sit by my father's side. There were cheers and laughter, and everyone came to congratulate me, but it was too much to process. It is still too much to process. Is this real? Can I really become a scribe?

hesitate stop briefly
an account a description
fluently clearly and well
the weight of the world a heavy feeling

Day one, first month of the harvesting season

It's been a few weeks since the banquet. I am going to school now, and Nebamun is not only my friend; he is my classmate. He is still better than I am at everything we try, but I'm learning a lot and catching up to him and the rest of the class. The teachers say I'm good with numbers, so I'm concentrating on that part. Father has told me what happened before the banquet. After my brother left, when he and Mother talked to me about taking over the family's business, he noticed the formal obedience in my response. He said he doesn't want either of his sons to take a job **with resignation**; he wants us to love what we do and get the respect we deserve through that.

with resignation because he has to

Father remembered seeing my attempts at writing and noticing I had an ability for **hieroglyphics**. So he took my case to Nebamun's father, who is **an influential person** in our community. My case was discussed at the school, and it was decided that my skills should be directed to what I could do best. I was worried about Father's workshop, but he told me my brother would be coming back to have a second chance to learn the family's trade. Father says my brother can learn to supervise and help Mother with the business side of things instead of doing crafts, which he doesn't like as much. He loves talking to customers in the market and **negotiating prices**. My brother is **thrilled** to be coming home to the family again. I am starting to do what I love, too, and I will honor my family by becoming a great scribe. I will probably be able to work with my friend Nebamun in the future. I am glad I get to be one of those rare cases, like the girl at school who became a doctor, where our skill is recognized and respected and we get the help of others to become our best selves. ❖

an influential person someone people respect; a powerful person

negotiating prices trying to get a good deal

thrilled very happy

▶ **Before You Continue**

1. **Plot** How are the conflicts in this story resolved? What are the feelings of the main characters in the end?

2. **Ask Questions** What did you learn about Nebamun and his family? Connect details in the text to answer the question.

Meet the Author

LAURA A. MEZA

Laura Meza always had a passion for writing, but when she was growing up she wrote mostly for herself, keeping a journal for many years to note her thoughts, feelings, and experiences. Later on, she started writing fiction, poems, and articles to share with others, mainly as a hobby but also to contribute to textbooks and publications for teachers or students. For her, the best thing about writing is the possibility of playing with words and learning about the subjects she has to research to create exciting or inspiring stories. What types of books would you enjoy writing?

Writing Tip

In "Ahmes's Journal," the author uses vivid words to help readers imagine the setting of the story. For instance, "the light was shining low over the water, making it look like a golden mirror," and "beads and other embellishments glittered on everyone's clothing." Write a description of a place using vivid words to bring the scene to life. Think about how vivid verbs, adjectives, and adverbs can create more dimension in your description.

Key Words

chamber	peer
command	perspective
consider	plunder
contribute	procession
hieroglyphics	significant
impact	

Talk About It 💬

1. "Ahmes's Journal" is a fictional diary. How would the story have changed if it had been written as a regular fiction story?

2. Reread the scene on page 186 in which Ahmes meets Nebamun. How does this scene **contribute** to the overall development of the plot?

3. How does learning about a young girl breaking tradition and becoming a doctor change Ahmes's **perspective** about his life and world?

4. Explain how Ahmes changes from the beginning to the end of the diary. Use text evidence to support your conclusion.

5. Compare your life with details of Ahmes's life. How does making connections help you answer questions or understand more about the story?

6. How do the illustrations and details about the setting contribute to your understanding of ancient Egyptian life? Cite at least three examples from the diary entries to support your ideas.

Write About It ✏️

Think about Nebamun's response to Ahmes's problems. Write a personal letter from Nebamun to a friend to describe the events from his perspective. Use at least three **Key Words**.

Dear Friend,

    Some days ago, I made a new friend when I was hunting wild birds in the marshes. His name is Ahmes...

Plot

Use a plot diagram to record the main events in "Ahmes's Journal" and how the characters respond to these events. Include the turning point and the resolution.

Plot Diagram

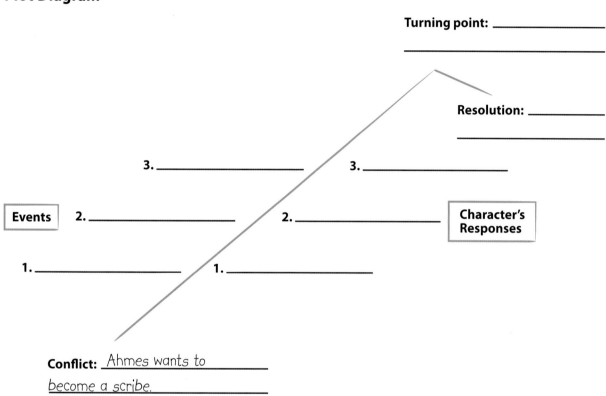

Turning point: _____

_____

Resolution: _____

_____

3. _____   3. _____

Events   2. _____   2. _____   **Character's Responses**

1. _____   1. _____

Conflict: _Ahmes wants to_
become a scribe.

Use your plot diagram to retell the story events to a partner. Explain how the characters' responses to different events help move the plot forward.

Fluency

Practice reading with expression. Rate your reading.

Talk Together

How does "Ahmes's Journal" bring the past to life through its entries?
Discuss your ideas with a partner. Use **Key Words**.

Compound Words

A **compound word** is made up of two or more base words. Sometimes you can define a compound word if you know the meanings of the smaller words.

EXAMPLE

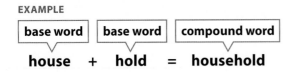

| base word | base word | compound word |

house + hold = household

Using the meanings of the words *house* and *hold*, you can figure out that *household* means "things held in a house" or "things related to a house."

Here are some strategies to figure out the meanings of compound words:

- Break down the word into its smaller parts, and think about the meaning of each part. Then put the meanings together and see if the new word makes more sense.

- Look for nearby context clues that might give hints about the word's meaning.

Try It

Read the sentences. Then answer the questions. Use the strategies above.

> In the morning, after having a large piece of <u>homemade</u> bread, a few dates, and some milk, I went to the marshes with my brother. We started out in the boat just after <u>sunrise</u>, when the light was shining low over the water, making it look like a golden mirror.

1. **What is the best meaning for the compound word <u>homemade</u>?**

   A   made near a home

   B   made for family members

   C   made at home

   D   made locally

2. **What is the best meaning for the compound word <u>sunrise</u>?**

   A   the time when the sun is overhead

   B   the time when the sun comes up

   C   the time when people see the sun

   D   the time when the sun sets

from *The Golden Goblet*

BY
Eloise Jarvis McGraw
ILLUSTRATED BY JOEL SPECTOR

*T*here was a silence that seemed as long as time itself to Ranofer, who lay in a tight ball, dizzy with fright, on the floor of the passage. Then he heard Gebu's voice in the second room, sounding unconcerned as ever.

"It was nothing. You're afraid of **your own shadow**."

"I tell you I heard a sound," the voice of Wenamon insisted.

"There is no one here but us and the dead. **Make haste** with those boxes, now."

Slowly, uncertainly, Ranofer rose to his knees, then stood. No one here? But what was that face he had seen? Trembling, he **peered** again through the opening, and met the same pair of eyes. This time, though he shrank back involuntarily, he realized that they did not move, did not live. They were the inlaid glass eyes of a life-sized wooden statue, and he saw now that they had been partially smashed, as if from **the blow of a dagger hilt**. Gebu and Wenamon had wanted no gaze upon them as they went about their evil work, especially the gaze of this watchful *ushabti* placed here as servant and **guardian** of the dead.

your own shadow everything
Make haste Hurry
the blow of a dagger hilt being hit with the handle of a large knife
guardian guard; protector

▶ **Before You Continue**
1. **Explain** Why is Ranofer frightened? List at least two reasons from the text.
2. **Ask Questions** What question do you have about the *ushabti*? Combine details or read on to find an answer.

201

Nervously Ranofer examined the **figure** more closely, and his fear of its **vengeance** changed to an unexpected pity. It was the statue of a slim and lovely servant girl, wearing a painted white dress and a painted gilt necklace, steadying a box on one shoulder and carrying a painted wooden duck by its feet in her other hand. Her expression was one of **serenity** and joy, and the sculptor who carved her had been a master. Now her clear, wide eyes were cloudy and blinded by the blow that had splintered them; her beauty was marred and her usefulness as a watchful guardian ended. It was like seeing some innocent, happy creature lying murdered, victim of Gebu's **callous** greed.

Ranofer's gaze turned from her to move in wonder about the rest of the **chamber**, which was dimly illumined by the glow of the torch from the next room. As he looked a strange emotion took possession of him. Beyond and around the graceful statue were articles of household furniture, arranged as in a beautiful home. There were armchairs and beds of carved wood decorated with gold, there were alabaster honey jars, painted boxes resting on delicately wrought ivory legs. There was a wicker trunk ventilated by little slatted openings, through which the fragrance of the perfumed garments within escaped into the room. There were winecups arranged on shelves, there were scent jars and jeweled collars and arm bands. Everywhere was the gleam of gold.

figure statue
vengeance revenge; anger
serenity peacefulness
callous selfish

It was not the gold, however, that held Ranofer's gaze and drew him slowly through the jagged entrance to stand, silent and awed, within the Precious Habitation. It was the garlands of flowers, only a little withered, as if placed here in love and grief only yesterday, and the sight of a worn oaken staff leaning against the wall, of two pairs of sandals, a new and an old, of favorite joints of meat placed neatly in boxes as if for a journey. Whatever he had expected, it was not this intimate look of home, of a well-loved room to which its owner might at any moment return. Whatever horrors haunted the passage, they were not here, in this quiet **sanctuary**.

Who was the owner? Ranofer's eyes searched farther, and halted in surprise. There were two owners. Slowly, soundlessly, he crossed the **chamber** to the pair of silver-inlaid coffins, on the lids of which were sculptured in gold the figures of their occupants, a man and a woman. They lay as if sleeping, side by side, their folded hands **eloquent of** the same defenseless trust that had caused them to order a sweet-faced servant girl as their only guardian. As Ranofer looked into their quiet golden faces the stealthy sounds of **plundering** in the next room became horrible to him. For the first time he fully understood this crime.

He straightened, all his fear gone and in its place hot fury. Those merciless and wicked ones!—to break into this sacred place and steal the treasures meant to comfort this old couple through their Three Thousand Years! Whether rich gold or worn-out sandals, these things belonged to them, no living human had a right to set foot in this chamber, not even the son of Thutra, who meant no harm. Almost, he could hear the helpless fluttering of these Old Ones' frightened **bas**. So strong was the sensation that he dropped to his knees in profound apology for his own **intrusion**. As he did so he saw something else, a stack of wine jars just beyond one of the coffins. They were capped with linen and sealed with clay, and pressed into the clay was a mark as well known to Ranofer as it was to everyone else in Egypt. It was the personal seal of the great noble, Huaa, only two years dead, the beloved father of Queen Tiy.

sanctuary place of rest
eloquent of showing
bas souls; spirits
intrusion entry

▶ **Before You Continue**

1. **Setting** Describe the tomb. What does this setting show about life in ancient Egypt?

2. **Ask Questions** Why do Ranofer's feelings change as he examines the tomb? Combine details to figure out the answer.

Shocked to his very toes, Ranofer scrambled up and retreated a few respectful steps, involuntarily stretching out his hands toward the coffins **in the gesture of homage**. Here lay Huaa and his cherished wife Tuaa, the parents of the queen of Egypt. And here he stood, an insignificant nobody, daring to gaze into their faces! He was acutely, desperately embarrassed; he felt like a **dusty urchin** trespassing in a palace, which he was. Worse, at any moment those thieves would be in here to wreck and **pillage**, to tear the gold trim from chairs and chests, to snatch the jewel boxes, to break open the beautiful coffins and even strip the wrappings from the royal mummies themselves in search of golden amulets. It must not happen. These Old Ones should have someone grand and fierce to protect them.

They have only me, Ranofer thought. I must do something—anything—go fetch help . . .

in the gesture of homage to show his
respect for them
dusty urchin poor boy
pillage plunder; steal

He turned and started swiftly toward the entrance hole, too swiftly, for his elbow grazed a little inlaid table and tilted the alabaster vase upon it. He clutched at it wildly but it fell, shattering on the stone floor with a crash that echoed like the very sound of doom.

The small noises in the **chamber** beyond ceased instantly. Ranofer breathed a prayer to Osiris and flung himself behind the coffins, which was all he had time to do before the torch and Gebu's murderous face appeared in the doorway.

"*Ast!*" came Wenamon's hiss. "I told you we were not alone!"

"We will be soon," Gebu answered in tones that **turned Ranofer cold**. He could see their two shadows on the wall, black and clear-cut: Gebu's bulky one, Wenamon's, thin and vulture-shaped, behind it. The shadows moved, rippled in deadly silence along the wall, leaped crazily to the rough ceiling and down again as the two began methodically to search the room. The dancing black shapes advanced relentlessly toward the coffins, looming huge as giants as they came nearer. Ranofer's hand groped out blindly and closed on a small heavy object that felt like a jewel box. At that instant Gebu's **rage-distorted** face was thrust over the coffin.

Ranofer lunged to his feet and hurled the box with all his strength.

There was a glittering shower of gems as the box struck Gebu full in the eyes, **jarring** the torch from his hand. He gave a hoarse cry and staggered backward into Wenamon, who began to scream and curse as he fought the flame that was licking upwards into his cloak. In that one instant of confusion Ranofer saw his chance. He seized the nearest wine jar and aimed it straight at the blaze. There was a splattering crash and the torch hissed out, plunging the chamber into darkness. With the reek of wine and scorched cloth rising strong about him, Ranofer leaped for the far wall, feeling frantically along it for the entrance hole. Behind him the dark was **hideous with** yells and curses, with the sounds of splintering wood and jewelry crushed under foot as the two thieves plunged this way and that over the wine-slippery floor in search of him.

turned Ranofer cold scared Ranofer
rage-distorted angry; furious
jarring knocking
hideous with filled with angry

▶ **Before You Continue**

1. **Plot** What important decision does Ranofer make in the tomb? How does this affect his actions?
2. **Summarize** In your own words, explain how Ranofer defends himself.

Where, in the name of all the gods, was the hole?

His fingers met a jagged bit of plaster and, beside it, empty space. In an instant he was through the hole and stumbling along the black passage, bent double under its crowding roof, banging and bumping into its **roughhewn** walls, but running, flying away from the death behind him. The sounds of rage faded as he ran, grew fainter with every bend, then suddenly grew louder. The thieves had found the wall opening, too, and were after him, in the passage. He scrambled around a curve, almost fell, dashed on again and **brought up with** a stunning impact against solid wall. Walls on three sides of him? Was he trapped? He wasted precious moments seeking a way around the obstruction; then his hand touched a rough shelf of stone. A step! He had reached the bottom of the entrance shaft much sooner than he had expected, for his **headlong flight** back had **consumed** far less time than his first cautious, crawling journey.

He clawed at the wall, found step after narrow step and hoisted his trembling body up them one by one. As he put his weight on the last one it crumbled under him. In a panic he flung both arms over the top of the shaft and for a terrible moment hung there, then wriggling, straining, pushing, he was over the top and through the crevice in the rocks.

The sunlight hit him like a blow. Half blind and shaking all over, he could think only of that last crumbled step and what it could mean to him. The thieves might climb past by jumping and then wriggling as he had done, but they could not get out if the top of the shaft were solidly blocked. They would have nothing to stand on to shove away the stones. He could hear stumbling, rapid footsteps approaching the bottom of the shaft, and Gebu's enraged voice bellowing his name; but already he was grabbing up rocks as fast as he could move, his eyes squinted

roughhewn unfinished
brought up with was stopped suddenly by
headlong flight run
consumed taken

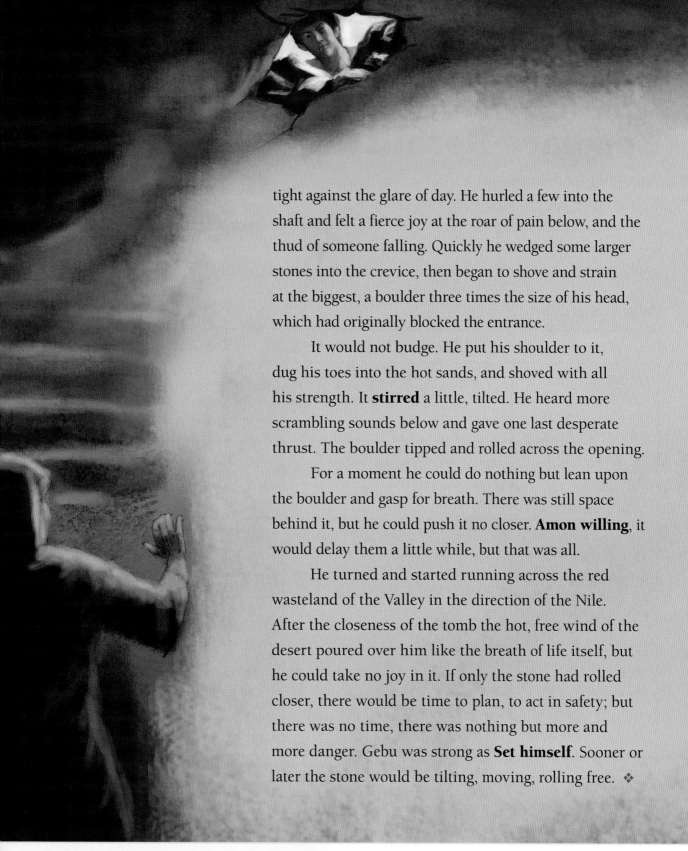

tight against the glare of day. He hurled a few into the shaft and felt a fierce joy at the roar of pain below, and the thud of someone falling. Quickly he wedged some larger stones into the crevice, then began to shove and strain at the biggest, a boulder three times the size of his head, which had originally blocked the entrance.

It would not budge. He put his shoulder to it, dug his toes into the hot sands, and shoved with all his strength. It **stirred** a little, tilted. He heard more scrambling sounds below and gave one last desperate thrust. The boulder tipped and rolled across the opening.

For a moment he could do nothing but lean upon the boulder and gasp for breath. There was still space behind it, but he could push it no closer. **Amon willing**, it would delay them a little while, but that was all.

He turned and started running across the red wasteland of the Valley in the direction of the Nile. After the closeness of the tomb the hot, free wind of the desert poured over him like the breath of life itself, but he could take no joy in it. If only the stone had rolled closer, there would be time to plan, to act in safety; but there was no time, there was nothing but more and more danger. Gebu was strong as **Set himself**. Sooner or later the stone would be tilting, moving, rolling free. ❖

---

stirred moved
Amon willing If the god, Amon, helped him
Set himself the Egyptian god Set

▶ **Before You Continue**

1. **Figurative Language** What does "The sunlight hit him like a blow" mean? Use context clues to figure out an answer.
2. **Character** Describe some of Ranofer's traits based on his actions and decisions in the tomb.

Respond and Extend

Key Words

chamber	peer
command	perspective
consider	plunder
contribute	procession
hieroglyphics	significant
impact	

Compare Details

The authors of "Ahmes's Journal" and "The Golden Goblet" both use historical facts and fictional details to write about similar topics and themes. Work with a partner to complete a comparison chart with details from both texts. Then use the information to synthesize, or put together, a general idea about ancient Egyptian life.

Comparison Chart

	"Ahmes's Journal"	"The Golden Goblet"
Genre		Historical fiction
Narrator's Point of View	First-person: Ahmes writes about his own thoughts and feelings.	
Historical Facts		
Fictional Details		
Theme		

Talk Together

How do the historical fiction story and the fictional diary bring the past to life? What **perspective** do they give you that informational texts like "The Valley of the Kings" and "Animals Everlasting" do not? Use **Key Words** and evidence from the selections to talk about your ideas with a partner.

Modals

A **modal** works together with another verb. The **main verb** tells the action. The modal supports the main verb's meaning.

Grammar Rules **Modals**

Some **modals** change the meaning of the **main verb**.

• Use **can** to tell what someone or something is able to do.	We **can learn** about the ancient Egyptians.
• Use **could**, **may**, or **might** to tell what is possible or permitted.	Experts **may discover** the person's name. They **might tell** us about the mummy.
• Use **should** to tell what is good for someone to do.	We **should care** for ancient artifacts.
• Use **must** to tell what someone has to or needs to do.	We **must do** all we can to protect the tombs.
• Use **would** to tell what someone is willing to do.	I **would like** to visit an ancient tomb.

Read Modals

Writers often use helping verbs to give advice or guidance. Read this passage based on "Ahmes's Journal." What modals can you find?

> "Very well, then," said Nebamun's father. "You should go to school and study so that you can learn those things, and I hope you can become as good a scribe as my son will be." I could not believe my luck!

Write Modals

Reread pages 203–204 of "The Golden Goblet" to find Ranofer's thoughts about plundering tombs. Write a paragraph that explains why plundering a tomb is wrong. Include at least two sentences that use modals. Then compare your sentences with a partner's.

Write as a Researcher

Write a Research Report ✎

Write a report that brings to life some aspect of ancient Egypt. Place your reports in a class book called *Bringing Ancient Egypt to Life*.

Study a Model

A research report is a nonfiction report that gives information about a topic. But it is more than a collection of facts. It is also a way of sharing the conclusions you make based on those facts. You gather information, think about what you've learned, and describe what it all means.

Read Julia's report about the pharaoh Hatshepsut.

The title and introduction capture the reader's interest and tell what the report is about.

Hatshepsut: The Woman Pharaoh of Egypt
by Julia Nguyen

An ancient Egyptian statue depicts a pharaoh. All the usual signs are there: the figure wears a pharaoh's striped headdress and traditional false beard. But it has the body of a woman! It is the pharaoh Hatshepsut. **Hatshepsut, who lived about 3,500 years ago, was an unusual woman who became a powerful ruler.**

The introduction also presents the **central idea**.

Each paragraph has a **topic sentence** that supports the central idea.

The path Hatshepsut took to become pharaoh was unheard of for a woman in ancient Egypt. She was the daughter of the pharaoh Thutmose I and the wife of his successor, Thutmose II. **When her husband died**, his son, Thutmose III, was supposed to inherit the throne. But Thutmose III was still a child, so Hatshepsut stepped in as temporary ruler. **After seven successful years**, Hatshepsut seized power for herself. She was crowned king of all of Egypt, and Thutmose III was pushed aside.

The report has a clear organization. Events are presented in the **chronological sequence** in which they happened.

The writer supports her ideas with **facts and details**.

The Egyptians seemed to accept Hatshepsut as their king, and she enjoyed a peaceful and successful 21-year reign. She expanded trade into parts of Africa and the Middle East. This brought riches to her country and her people. Hatshepsut also built many temples throughout Egypt. One of her most magnificent temples still stands at Deir el Bahri.

No one knows how Hatshepsut's reign ended, but when it did, Thutmose III came to power. At some point during Thutmose III's reign, there was an effort to destroy statues and images of Hatshepsut. Her name was removed from official records. According to author Chip Brown, the work to remove Hatshepsut from history "was careful and precise."

Not all evidence of Hatshepsut was erased, however. In the nineteenth century, Egyptologists succeeded in deciphering hieroglyphics that told about Hatshepsut. Today people are able to marvel at the achievements of this amazing woman pharaoh.

The bibliography on the final page lists the sources Julia used. Julia conducted her research by reading these sources to gather the information she used for her report.

Bibliography

Brown, C. (2009, April). The King Herself. *National Geographic Magazine, 88–111.*

Tyldesley, Joyce. (2014). Hatshepsut. In *Encyclopædia Britannica.* Retrieved from https://www.britannica.com/biography/Hatshepsut

History.com Editors. (2009). *Hatshepsut.* Retrieved from https://www.history.com/topics/ancient-history/hatshepsut

Prewrite

1. **Choose a Central Idea** Think about what you have learned about ancient Egypt. What aspect of ancient Egyptian civilization is most interesting to you? Work with a partner to brainstorm and discuss ideas. Narrow your topic to one that you can cover well in a short report.

2. **List Your Research Questions** What do you already know about your topic? What do you want to find out? With your partner, think of questions you could use to guide your research. You can add to this list as you learn more.

Research Questions

- Who was Hatshepsut?
- How did she come to power?
- What are some achievements of her reign?
- How do we know about her today?

---

3. **Create a Research Plan** A research report must contain information from several different sources. Your research plan contains your questions and your ideas about the sources you can use to answer them. Your sources may include both print and digital texts and visual information. Determine the search terms and methods you will use for online research.

Topic: Hatshepsut

Text Sources	Visual Sources
• magazine article about Hatshepsut and her legacy • online encyclopedia entry about Hatshepsut	• photos of statues, temples, and other artifacts related to Hatshepsut • video about unsolved mysteries about Hatshepsut • a visit to a museum

Text sources are materials that you read online or in print. They include primary sources, such as letters and diaries, and secondary sources, such as nonfiction books, periodicals, websites, and reference books.

Visual information may be found online, in print, or in person. You can get visual information from viewing videos, photographs, charts, graphs, diagrams, and so on. A museum visit also provides visual information.

Gather Information

1. **Identify Credible Sources** Credible, or valid, sources are up to date and written or created by a group or person who is an expert on the topic. Be sure to assess the credibility of each source you find.

   Evaluate the accuracy and reliability of each source. The facts you find should match from source to source. Try to find each fact in two different sources.

   Review each source to locate information. Skim the tables of contents, headings, and pictures. On a website, check the menus and links.

2. **Record Sources** Use numbered index cards or create a searchable document or matrix on a computer to record important information about each source.

   Source Card

3. **Take Notes** Record important words, phrases, and ideas from your research in your own words. This is called *paraphrasing*. If you quote from your source or pick up anything word for word, use quotation marks and name the source.

   Include visuals in your report. Keep a separate file for any pictures, maps, or charts you may want to use. Be sure to record their sources.

   Note Card

   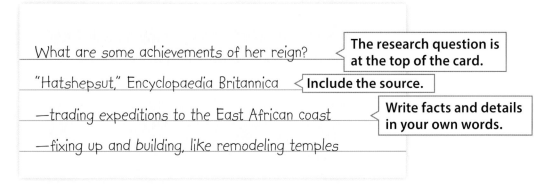

Get Organized

1. **Sort the Information** Use the research questions to sort your notes into categories. If you have a lot of information, create subcategories based on your main ideas. Group all of your information in a logical order.

2. **Organize Your Details** Use an outline or another graphic organizer to organize how you will present the information. Each category from your cards becomes a main idea. The details from each card support the main ideas.

Outline

Use Roman numerals for main ideas.

Use capital letters for supporting points. There must always be at least an A and a B.

Add more details using Arabic numbers (1, 2, 3).

I. Hatshepsut's path to power was unheard of.
  A. Daughter and wife of pharaoh
  B. Husband died, the son was supposed to rule
    1. The son was a child
    2. Hatshepsut became temporary ruler
  C. After 7 years, she seized power and became King
II. Hatshepsut had a peaceful and successful reign
  A. Expanded trade
  B. Built many temples

Draft

1. Use your outline or graphic organizer to guide you as you write. Begin with an introduction that tells what the report is about. Then write a paragraph for each main idea. Include visuals to help explain your ideas.

2. Put the rest of the information in your own words. Never copy directly from a source without giving proper credit. If you use another person's work without naming the source and using quotation marks, you claim that the ideas and words are all your own. This is called **plagiarizing**, and it's a type of stealing.

Revise

1. **Read, Retell, Respond** Read the draft of your report to a partner. Your partner listens and summarizes the main points of the report. Then discuss specific ways that you can improve your writing.

2. **Make Changes** Think about your draft and your partner's suggestions. Use revision marks to make your changes.

   - Are your facts presented in a logical order that your readers can follow? Move any that seem out of place.

     > She was crowned king of all of Egypt. ~~That was because~~ after seven years, Hatshepsut seized power for herself and Thutmose III was pushed aside.

   - Did you use your own words in each sentence? If not, make the sentence into a quote and name the source. Or rewrite the sentence in your own words.

     > She expanded trade into parts of Africa and the Middle East. ~~During her reign, she was responsible for the extension of trade into Eastern Africa and across the Sinai peninsula.~~

Edit and Proofread

Work with a partner to edit and proofread your research report. Carefully check all your facts, as well as names, dates, and numbers. Make sure direct quotes are in quotation marks. Also check to be sure you have used formal language throughout your report. Use revision marks to show your changes.

Present

1. **Make a Final Copy** Finalize your research report. Ask your teacher if there is a special format, or way of presenting your report, that you should use. At the end, add a bibliography to cite all of your sources.

2. **Share with Others** Present your paper as an oral report or multimedia slideshow. Include images you used. Then, with your classmates, collect your reports and publish them in a book called *Bringing Ancient Egypt to Life*.

Talk Together

In this unit you found many answers to the **Big Question**. Now use your concept map to discuss it with the class. List what this unit taught you about ancient Egypt.

KWL Chart

How can we bring the past to life?		
What I <u>Know</u> Already	What I <u>Want</u> to Know	What I <u>Learned</u>
People study Egyptian pyramids and mummies.	How can mummies help us learn about the past?	

Performance Task: Explanatory

Remember what you learned about ancient Egypt from reading the selections. Choose something about ancient Egypt that interests you, such as an archaeological site, an unusual custom, or a pharaoh. Write a blog entry that explains what you learned about this topic or person.

Checklist

Does your blog entry

- ✔ use text evidence from the selections about Egypt?
- ✔ clearly introduce the topic?
- ✔ include facts, definitions, details, or other information and examples from the sources?
- ✔ include precise language and transition words?

Share Your Ideas

Choose one of these ways to share your ideas about the **Big Question**.

Write It!

Write a Story

Pretend that you are an archaeologist. Write about discovering your first mummy. Where did you find the tomb and how did you find it? Describe what you see in the tomb including artifacts, artwork, and other clues about ancient Egyptian life. Include as many details as possible. Why is this discovery important?

Talk About It!

Conduct an Interview

In groups of three, conduct an interview with one character from "Ahmes's Journal" and one character from "The Golden Goblet." Decide who will be the interviewer and who will play the characters. Discuss what these characters might say to each other about living in ancient Egypt. Perform your interview for the class.

Do It!

Create a Photo-Essay

Find pictures on the Internet of objects that tell about life in ancient Egypt. Use presentation software to create a photo-essay slideshow. Write a few sentences about each object. How does each object help us understand the past?

This artwork depicts a pharaoh's family.

Write It!

Write a List

With a partner, write a list of modern-day objects you would want archaeologists to find years from now. What would these objects teach others about our society? Why is it important for future generations to find these items? Explain your list to the class.

Our Diverse EARTH

❓
BIG Question

Why is diversity important?

DHAKA, BANGLADESH
Children playing among mounds of rice covered at night
to protect the drying grains from moisture

Share What You Know

❶ **Draw** a beautiful place.

❷ **Explain** why it is special to you.

❸ **Share** your drawing with the class.

Language Frames

- We should _____ because _____.
- It is a fact that _____.
- According to experts, _____.

Make an Argument

Listen to the argument. Then use **Language Frames** to make your own argument about the best way to protect wildlife.

Save the Gray Wolf

Some people argue that wolves should be removed from the wild. That would be a tragic mistake. We should allow gray wolves to stay in their natural territory because they are an important part of a balanced ecosystem. Wolves prey on weaker animals like deer. As a result, populations of deer and other animals stay balanced—not too many and not too few. It is a fact that this makes the remaining animals stronger.

Ranchers argue that wolves should be removed because wolves kill their livestock. But that is not the answer. According to experts, a better solution is to teach ranchers how to live with wolves. Then ranchers will lose less livestock, and wolves may get the chance to make a comeback.

🔊 Key Words

Look at the photographs and read the text. Use **Key Words** and other words to talk about why we should protect animals.

Key Words

dependent
endangered
extinct
policy
recover
thrive

manatee

Problem

The number of manatees in the world is getting smaller, making them an **endangered** species. One cause for this change in numbers is boat traffic which may injure or kill manatees. If this does not improve, manatees may become **extinct** and no longer exist.

MANATEE ZONE
IDLE SPEED
NO WAKE
• ALL YEAR •
PERMIT NO 02-037   62N-22.011 FAC

Action

Manatees are **dependent** on humans because they need our help. We must change the boating **policies**, or laws, to protect manatees.

Solution

When manatees are protected, they will **thrive**, and their numbers will **recover** to the levels they were before.

Talk Together

What should people do to help endangered species thrive? Work with a partner to create an argument that includes a claim, reasons, and evidence. Use **Language Frames** from page 220 and **Key Words** to make your argument.

Author's Viewpoint

Many texts reflect an author's perspective, or **viewpoint**, about a topic. Sometimes, authors directly state their opinions. At other times, you must look for clues, such as the examples the author includes or the words the author chooses. For example, if an author uses the word *impact* to describe the way you affect the world, you can determine that the author believes you have the power to affect the world in an important way.

Look Into the Text

You wash your face, chat with your family, eat your breakfast, and jump on the school bus. Even before you get to school, you have **interacted** with many people and things. Believe it or not, all of the things you do—**your outdoor activities, what you eat and drink, how you travel from place to place**—have an **impact** on the world around you.

"The author includes many **examples** of ways we affect the world."

"Her **word choice** shows that the effect is serious and important."

Map and Talk

A viewpoint chart can help you keep track of words, phrases, and examples that reveal how an author feels about a topic.

Viewpoint Chart

Text Evidence	Author's Viewpoint
"Believe it or not, all of the things you do . . . have an impact on the world around you."	The author believes that your actions have strong, important effects on the world.

Talk Together

Do your actions impact the world around you? Discuss your opinions with a partner and record them on a viewpoint chart. List your strongest words and phrases as text evidence and record what they show about your viewpoint. Then use the chart to form an argument about the topic.

◄ᴏ More Key Words

Use these words to talk about "A Natural Balance" and "Mireya Mayor."

appeal
noun

An **appeal** is a serious request for help. The student made an **appeal** to his teacher for help with a project.

effective
adjective

Something that is **effective** has good results. An umbrella is **effective** for keeping dry in the rain.

factor
noun

A **factor** is something that can lead to a specific result. Heavy rains were a **factor** in the terrible flooding.

protection
noun

Protection keeps people, animals, and things safe. Helmets give **protection** to the bikers' heads.

sustain
verb

To **sustain** is to continue or keep up an action, event, or thing. The runner drinks lots of water to **sustain** her during the race.

Talk Together

Make a Word Map for each **Key Word**. Then compare your maps with a partner's.

Definition	Characteristics
a thing that keeps someone or something safe	provides safety, security
Word: protection	
A roof gives protection from rain.	A lamppost does not give protection from rain.
Examples	**Non-examples**

Learn to Make Connections

Did you ever read something that reminded you of something else? If you did, you made a connection that could help you better understand the text.

How to Make Connections

1. As you read, think about things that relate to the text.
   - **Self to Text (S-T):** Connect something in the text with your experience or knowledge.
   - **Text to Text (T-T):** Explain how the text connects to something else you have read or seen.
   - **Text to World (T-W):** Explain how the text connects to a problem or issue in the world.

2. Decide how each connection helps you better understand the text.

I read _____.

This reminds me of _____.

This helps me understand _____.

Here's how one student made a connection to a text.

Look Into the Text

All across Earth, humans are changing the environment in small and large ways. We cut down trees for lumber to build houses. We plow fields to grow crops. . . . These activities also affect nonliving things in the environment, such as soil and water.

I read a magazine article about how trees protect hills from landslides. (T-T)

"I read **a fact from the text**. This reminds me of **an article I read before**. This helps me understand why trees are important."

Making connections as you read can help you make sense of the author's viewpoint. It can also help make the text more understandable and meaningful to you.

Read the Web article and sample notes. Use **Language Frames** to make connections as you read. Talk with a partner about the connections you made.

Language Frames

I read _____ .

This reminds me of _____ .

This helps me understand _____ .

Web Article

Sea Turtle Conservation

https://eltngl.com/reachhigherseries

Sea Turtle Conservation

Sea Turtles | Species | Protection | Volunteer

Sea Turtles

Sea turtles are air-breathing reptiles that have lived on Earth for 110 million years. Yet, each of the world's seven species is now threatened or **endangered**.

Life Cycle Sea turtles spend almost their entire lives in the sea. Females come ashore to lay eggs. Although flippers are highly **effective** for swimming, they make moving on land difficult. A female must crawl across the sand to find a nesting spot that is far from the water's edge. There, she lays her eggs, buries them in the sand, and then crawls back to the sea.

After 60 to 90 days, the sea turtle hatchlings emerge. Only about two inches in length, the tiny creatures must dig out of the sand. Then they are **dependent** on instinct to find their way to the water. The trail to the sea offers little **protection**, and many hatchlings fall prey to sea birds and other animals. ◄

Threats Human actions are an important **factor** in the threats to sea turtles. For centuries, sea turtles have been hunted for their meat, eggs, and shells. Fishing nets and lines drown them. Beach activity damages nests and eggs. Furthermore, bright lights can distract hatchlings at night, leading them away from the water.

Solutions Many programs now exist to help **sustain** sea turtle populations. Several countries have banned the harvesting of sea turtles and the sale of turtle-related products. **Appeals** to coastal communities have helped reduce light pollution and raise awareness of nesting grounds. ◄

With careful planning, education, and environmental **policies**, there is hope that the sea turtle population will **recover** and **thrive** once more.

I read that tiny turtle hatchlings must dig their way out of their nests.

This reminds me of my experience struggling to dig through heavy sand. (S-T).

This helps me understand how difficult it is for small turtle hatchlings to emerge from their nests.

DO NOT DISTURB SEA TURTLE NEST VIOLATORS SUBJECT TO FINES AND IMPRISONMENT

◄ = a good place to stop and make a connection

225

Read an Environmental Report

Genre

Environmental reports are nonfiction. They give facts and information about environmental topics. Authors often inform or alert readers to issues that affect nature.

Text Features

Visual graphics present information in creative formats, such as charts, tables, diagrams, and lists. These may support the text or present new information in ways that are easy to understand.

This visual graphic shows three stages that happen when a species becomes extinct.

The Road to Extinction

Going
Threatened

Going
Endangered

Gone
Extinct

A Natural Balance

based on a book by Nora L. Deans

Green sea turtles swim off the coast of Bora Bora Island. These turtles are **endangered** in many countries.

▶ Set a Purpose
Learn why animals, plants, and humans need each other.

Some conservation efforts include relocating sea turtle eggs.

Our Effect on the Environment

Beep! Beep! Beep! Your alarm goes off, and you hop out of bed. You wash your face, chat with your family, eat your breakfast, and jump on the school bus. Even before you get to school, you have interacted with many people and things. Believe it or not, all of the things you do—your outdoor activities, what you eat and drink, how you travel from place to place—**have an impact on** the world around you.

The way we live our lives affects the environment. The environment is all of the living and nonliving things around you. All across Earth, humans are changing the environment in small and large ways. We cut down trees for lumber to build houses. We plow fields to grow crops. We pave roads and build parking lots. We pour waste into rivers, lakes, and oceans. We use giant nets and boats to catch huge numbers of fish. Activities like these affect plants and animals. These activities also affect nonliving things in the environment, such as soil and water.

A kayaker passes by trash along the shore of the Anacostia River near Washington, DC.

have an impact on affect or change

▶ **Before You Continue**

1. **Make Connections** According to the text, how do we affect the world around us? What does this remind you of?

2. **Details** What are two specific ways that humans change land and water? How does this impact the environment?

Are We Helping or Harming?

Sometimes our actions allow a certain plant or animal population—or the total number of individuals in a group—to get larger. For example, if you planted tulips in your yard, the tulip population in your area would increase. Or if you put seeds out for the birds in your area, the bird population might get larger.

Our activities can also lead to smaller plant and animal populations. What would happen to the plants and animals in a neighborhood park if the park were turned into an apartment building? They would either die or move some place else. Then the area's plant and animal populations would shrink.

Overhunting, pollution, and other activities sometimes cause the population of a species to become so small that it cannot survive. A species that is in danger of dying out is called an **endangered** species. When a species can no longer survive and dies out completely, it becomes **extinct**. A species that is extinct is gone forever.

▲ Drivers must learn to share the highway with black bears in Nevada.

The Road to Extinction

An easy way to remember the threats facing plants and animals today is HIPPO. It stands for:

- **Habitat loss**–cutting down trees and tearing up the land often leaves plants and animals with no place to live

- **Introduced species**–bringing in new life-forms that crowd out or feed on the ones that were there

- **Pollution**–chemicals and wastes that damage or even kill living things

- **Population growth**–more and more people who need more food and more land

- **Over-consumption**–hunting and harvesting more plants or animals than you need

What's Harming the Habitat?

The way we use or pollute natural resources, such as water or land, affects the environment. Several **factors** contribute to the loss of habitats. Habitats are the areas that support plant and animal populations.

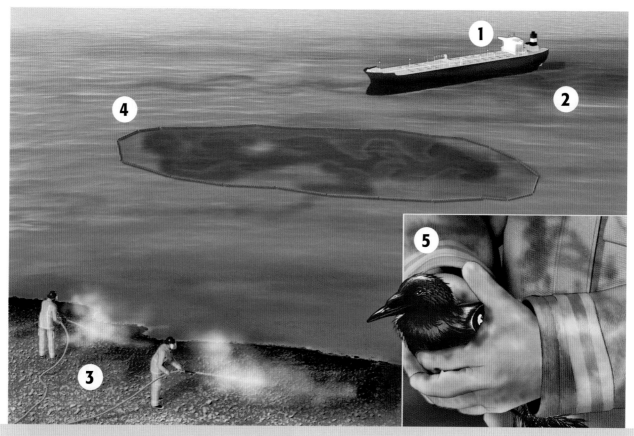

Oil spill emergency

1   Oil spills are major ocean disasters. An oil spill is what happens when a tanker, or large ship, carrying oil gets a hole in it and leaks the oil.

2   A large tanker gets stuck on shallow land. When crew members start to drive the tanker again, they can put a hole in it, leaking the oil.

3   As part of the clean-up effort, oily shore rocks and sand are rinsed with very hot water. Thousands of workers help clean up the spill.

4   **Containment booms** surround large areas of oil.

5   Oil-soaked birds are cleaned with **absorbent pads**. Some survive, but hundreds of thousands die. Sea otters, whales, and schools of fish also die.

Containment booms Floating materials that stop oil from spreading

absorbent pads cloths to soak up the oil

▶ **Before You Continue**

1. **Author's Viewpoint** What does the author think is harming our environment? Use evidence from the text to explain.

2. **Use Text Features** What information does the diagram show about the effects of oil spills on living and nonliving things?

231

Are We Solving the Problem?

As groups of plants and animals began to disappear, people began working on a **policy** to protect these species. In the early 1900s, some laws were passed to protect certain animals. However, the **big breakthrough** came in 1973. This is when the United States government passed the **Endangered** Species Act. This act lists species that are in danger of becoming **extinct**. The act also makes it illegal to disturb, harm, pursue, shoot, wound, kill, trap, capture, or collect any of the species on the list. The act protects not only the listed species but also the areas where they live. If a species is **dependent** on a certain habitat, that area needs to be protected, too.

Many species are on the list, but they're not all classified the same way. Species are listed as either "endangered" or "threatened." An endangered species is one in danger of becoming extinct. A threatened species is a species that could become endangered without **protection**.

The U.S. Fish and Wildlife Service (FWS) is the government agency that enforces the Endangered Species Act. Many of the scientists at FWS keep a close watch on endangered and threatened plants and animals. They track the populations of the species on the list. They also collect information about the areas where the species live.

If the collected information from the FWS shows that the population of a threatened species is steadily decreasing, the species could be reclassified as an endangered species. If the population of an endangered species gets larger, it could be downlisted. This means that it is moved one step down to the threatened species list. If the population of a species gets large enough, it could be removed from the list completely.

▼ A threatened species can become **endangered** without **protection**. An endangered species can become **extinct**.

The Road to Extinction

Going
Threatened

Going
Endangered

Gone
Extinct

---

big breakthrough most important change

Endangered Animals

▲ Black rhinoceros

▲ Mitchell's satyr butterfly

▲ Golden-shouldered parrot

Habitat loss is the most serious threat facing manatees today.

▶ **Before You Continue**

1. **Author's Viewpoint** What evidence from the text shows how the author feels about protecting habitats?

2. **Summarize** Tell in your own words what threats plants and animals face today.

For example, the bald eagle used to be listed as an **endangered** species. In 1963, there were only 400 pairs of these birds left. By 1995, after many recovery efforts, the bald eagle population had increased enough for the FWS to reclassify the bald eagle from "endangered" to "threatened." Due to government and volunteer efforts, there are about 10,000 pairs today. The bald eagle has now been removed from the endangered and threatened species lists.

Along with the FWS, additional organizations and individuals try to protect endangered species as well. Zoos and aquariums often work together to breed and raise rare and endangered animals. Botanical gardens and other groups raise rare and endangered plants. They also save their seeds.

Not everyone agrees about what is the best way to help an endangered species. Sometimes helping the animals interferes with people's jobs or activities. Like so many cases involving endangered species, survival means balancing the **protection** of endangered species with people's ways of life.

▲ The aloe's habitat is affected by burning and other kinds of habitat destruction.

▲ Orchid smuggling is leading to the loss of many kinds of wild orchids.

▲ The government began protecting the saguaro cactus when it started to disappear. This has prevented it from becoming **endangered**.

◄ On June 28, 2007, the bald eagle was taken off the Federal List of **Endangered** and Threatened Wildlife and Plants. The bald eagle will still be protected by the Bald and Golden Eagle **Protection** Act.

How Well Are We Doing?

Good News

- Thanks to the **Endangered** Species Act, conservation groups and government agencies are working together to protect endangered species.

- Twenty-seven species on the endangered species list, including the gray whale and American alligator, have **recovered** enough to be taken off the list.

- Better **field research techniques** give us faster and better data about endangered species.

- Many groups, including zoos and aquariums that breed rare and endangered species, are trying to help many species survive.

Bad News

- There are many disagreements between organizations and the general public about how best to take care of endangered species.

- More research has to be done before hundreds of plants and animals can be included on the endangered or threatened species lists.

- Since being listed on the endangered species list, 10 species have become **extinct**. Some scientists think that thousands of unlisted species are becoming extinct each year.

- The presence of an endangered species may **halt a construction project**, cause people to lose their jobs, or even threaten humans' way of life.

field research techniques ways of studying nature

halt a construction project stop work at a building project

▶ **Before You Continue**

1. **Author's Viewpoint** How does the author feel about animals becoming **extinct**? How do you know?

2. **Make Connections** What connection can you make to the facts about the bald eagle populations?

235

A Balancing Act

Wolf Number 9 waits in a pen before her release into Yellowstone.

In 1995, fourteen gray wolves were captured in Canada and moved to Yellowstone National Park in the United States. An important female wolf in this group was called Number 9 by the Yellowstone biologists. She and her mate, Number 10, were **expecting a litter of pups** when Number 10 was killed by hunters.

Just after Number 10 died, Number 9 gave birth to eight pups. They were the first wolf pups born in Yellowstone in more than 60 years. Although her new life in Yellowstone had a hard beginning, Number 9 was able to **thrive** in her new home. During her lifetime, she has given birth to at least six litters of pups.

expecting a litter of pups going to have babies

"If I were going to make a statue to commemorate the wolf reintroduction, it would be a statue of Number 9," says Doug Smith, the biologist in charge of the wolf relocation. "She has **single-handedly** put this population back on its feet."

The Hunters and the Hunted

Gray wolves like Number 9 once roamed throughout North America. Wolves live in packs, or groups, of about six to twenty animals. Each member in a wolf pack helps the group survive. They work together to raise young wolf pups, protect the pack, and find food.

Gray wolves are predators that hunt a variety of prey, such as bison, elk, deer, and moose. At one time, the populations of wolves and their prey were in a natural balance. This means the populations were not too large or too small, and each species was able to survive.

The delicate balance between predator and prey was **disrupted** when European settlers came to North America. Soon, due to human hunters, wolves and many other animals began to disappear. Settlers killed more than 60 million bison. They also killed millions of elk, deer, and other wildlife. The wolves' natural prey became harder to find.

Wolf packs began to hunt livestock, such as cattle and sheep. People depended on that livestock for food, goods, or money. Wolves were then seen as troublesome, and hunters killed the wolves by the thousands. Government agencies even paid hunters bounties, or cash awards, for wolves that were shot.

The government once paid bounties to hunters who shot wolves.

single-handedly by herself
disrupted changed in a negative way

▶ **Before You Continue**

1. **Explain** Why do wolves and their prey need to be in a natural balance?

2. **Author's Viewpoint** What are the author's views on the European settlers? Use evidence from the text to support your answer.

gray wolf

A gray wolf captures its prey.

Making a Return

By the end of the 1930s, most of the gray wolves that once lived in the United States were gone. In the 1960s, the only gray wolves in the U.S. (not including Alaska) were a small number that still lived on either an island in Lake Superior or in Minnesota. By 1965, the government stopped paying wolf bounties. By then, the gray wolf population was in serious trouble.

After the **Endangered** Species Act was passed in 1973, the gray wolf was classified as an endangered species in 48 states. In 1995, biologists from FWS began the project to reintroduce gray wolves to Yellowstone. The scientists **got permits** to move 31 gray wolves from Canada: 14 were relocated in 1995, and 17 more moved in 1996.

Before releasing the wolves into the park, the biologists attached electronic collars around their necks. The scientists also took careful measurements of each wolf's length, weight, the size of its teeth, and other physical characteristics. These data allowed the scientists to study each wolf and keep track of the entire wolf population.

Today, there are between 400–450 wolves in the **Yellowstone recovery area**. With success, however, also came problems. As the wolves in Yellowstone multiplied, they split into new packs. The packs spread out, and each **claimed its own territory**. Some of the land that the wolves claimed was outside of the park on land owned by ranchers.

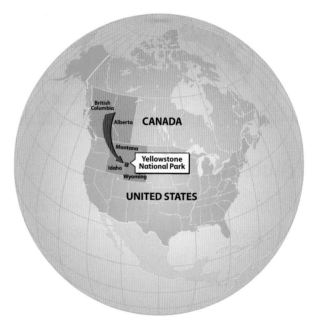

▲ **The route the wolves traveled to Yellowstone**

got permits were allowed
Yellowstone recovery area part of Yellowstone where the wolves were placed
claimed its own territory chose a different place to live

▶ **Before You Continue**

1. **Use Text Features** What part of the text does the map support? How does the map give information in a different way than the text?

2. **Make Connections** How can you help threatened or **endangered** species?

Trouble on the Ranch

"I never thought the wolf reintroduction was a good idea—they're killers no matter what." These are the words of one rancher **opposed to** the release of the wolves. Many other ranchers felt the same way.

Ranchers are in the business of raising and selling cattle, sheep, and other livestock. On a ranch, losing an animal to a wolf attack is a serious matter. More than 35,000 elk and other prey roam inside Yellowstone, and the wolves are free to hunt these animals. However, wolves sometimes hunt livestock outside the boundaries of the park. Since the gray wolf was an **endangered** species, ranchers worried about how they would be able to protect their livestock. The ranchers felt the wolves threatened their way of life. They wanted

opposed to who did not agree with

Protesters demonstrate against wolves in Ronan, Montana.

the wolves removed. An organization called the American Farm Bureau Federation represented the ranchers and worked to stop the wolf reintroduction program.

"We had one Farm Bureau member that had at one point this year 59 **head of ewes** and lambs killed," said Karen Henry, a rancher and president of the Wyoming Farm Bureau in 1997. "They took the wolf back to Yellowstone, and days after it was released, it was back there killing again—and killed an additional 15."

Each time livestock were killed by wolves, scientists investigated to find out which wolf or wolves had been involved. Researchers tried moving problem wolves to distant wilderness areas. This didn't always work.

Finding New Answers

Over the past several years, many steps have been taken to protect ranchers' livestock. When wolves repeatedly hunt livestock, the problem wolves are killed. Conservation organizations, like the Defenders of Wildlife, pay ranchers for the livestock they lose to wolf attacks. Some ranchers have also chosen to move **their grazing lands** to areas farther away from the wolves. Like so many other cases involving **endangered** species, survival for all means finding a balance between needs.

The gray wolf is still an endangered species that needs **protection**. Fortunately, the offspring of Number 9 continue to **thrive** in Yellowstone today. Through the hard work and compromises of many people, the wolves are again finding a place in the United States. ❖

head of ewes female sheep
their grazing lands the places where their livestock eat

▶ **Before You Continue**
1. **Explain** What happened during the wolf reintroduction that helped ranchers?
2. **Make Connections** How do the ranchers' problems with the wolves remind you of other world events? Explain.

Think and Respond

Talk About It

1. "A Natural Balance" is an environmental report. Choose one visual graphic from the report and explain how it presents information that helped you better understand what you read.

2. What is the author's purpose in writing the report? How **effective** is the author in meeting this purpose? Cite text evidence in your answer.

3. Review the visual graphic of the oil spill on page 231. What words and examples does the author include that explains her viewpoint about oil spills?

4. Animal populations can be classified as "threatened" or "**endangered**." Why is the difference in these terms important?

5. How do humans affect the natural balance of nature in positive and negative ways? Use specific examples from the text to support your response.

6. Do we provide adequate **protection** for animals and their habitats? Make an argument, using text evidence to support your claim.

Write About It

Write a brochure that could be placed near the habitat of one of the animals from "A Natural Balance." Explain why the animal needs help and what visitors to the area can do to protect the animal. Use at least three **Key Words** and include text evidence to support your ideas.

Manatee Habitat

Manatees are on the Endangered Species List. Help us keep them from going extinct!

It's illegal to:
- pursue
- wound

Author's Viewpoint

Use a viewpoint chart to record specific text evidence that reveals how the author of "A Natural Balance" feels about the environment.

Viewpoint Chart

Text Evidence	Author's Viewpoint
"Believe it or not, all of the things you do . . . have an impact on the world around you."	The author believes that your actions have strong, important effects on the world.

Use your viewpoint chart to help you summarize the author's main argument to a partner. Explain how the author's viewpoint is conveyed in the text and how she uses examples and chooses words that support her claims.

Fluency

Practice reading with phrasing. Rate your reading.

Talk Together

How does "A Natural Balance" show the value of diversity in nature? Discuss your ideas with a partner. Use **Key Words** and cite evidence from the text to support your ideas.

243

Prefixes and Base Words

A **prefix** is a word part that is added to the beginning of a **base word**. To find the meaning of a word with a prefix, think about what each word part means.

EXAMPLES

The prefix *inter-* means "among; between."

prefix	base word

inter- + act = interact

The prefix *dis-* means "opposite."

prefix	base word

dis- + appear = disappear

Prefix	Meaning	Examples
en-	to put in	enforce, enlist
in-	not	independent, ineffective
over-	too much	over-consumption, overhunting

The chart above shows more prefixes and their meanings. Based on the chart, what do you think the word *overestimate* means?

Try It

Read the sentences. Then answer the questions. Use the chart to help you.

Some <u>endangered</u> species are in trouble of becoming extinct. People need to improve <u>ineffective</u> laws and policies to help these struggling populations.

1. **Look for the prefix *en-*. What is the best meaning for the word <u>endangered</u>?**

   A put in danger

   B causing danger

   C saving from danger

   D classified as dangerous

2. **Look for the prefix *in-*. What is the best meaning for the word <u>ineffective</u>?**

   A not effective

   B very effective

   C used to be effective

   D will become effective

Making Connections You read about the importance of a natural balance. Now read about an explorer who is working to restore a natural balance in rainforests.

Genre An **online article** gives information about a topic. It can include links to other Web pages.

MIREYA MAYOR
EXPLORER/CORRESPONDENT

Mireya Mayor surveys a rainforest in Madagascar.

Emerging Explorers
National Geographic's Next Generation

OUR EXPLORERS   ABOUT THE PROGRAM

MIREYA MAYOR
EXPLORER/CORRESPONDENT

» J. MICHAEL FAY
CONSERVATIONIST

» SALIMA IKRAM
ARCHAEOLOGIST

» JOSEPH LEKUTON
TEACHER

» MIREYA MAYOR
**EXPLORER/
CORRESPONDENT**

"The rainforest appears to be a gigantic, green **mishmash** of unknowns. We are still discovering new species and who knows what else might be out there. But we do know that every tree and creature in it plays a vital role in our existence. Ensuring their survival helps to ensure ours."

Mireya Mayor has slept in the rainforest among poisonous snakes. She has been chased by gorillas, elephants, and leopards. She has even swum with great white sharks! Mayor is a city girl and a former NFL cheerleader. How did she find herself as an explorer in situations like this?

It all began in college. Mayor began studying **primates**. "I was **seized** by the fact that some of these incredible animals are **on the verge of** extinction. And they had never been studied. In some cases not even a mere photograph existed to show their existence. I asked more questions. It became clear to me that much about our natural world still remained a mystery." Mayor decided to dedicate her life to solving that mystery.

Today, Mayor is a Fulbright scholar and a National Science Foundation Fellow. She also appears as a host on the National Geographic *Wild Nights* television series. Each expedition allows

mishmash mixture
primates gorillas and other
    animals like them
seized very interested
on the verge of near

MIREYA MAYOR
EXPLORER/CORRESPONDENT

Click on map for detail

Mayor to teach viewers about a different species of animal that needs our help.

For example, one of Mayor's National Geographic TV expeditions allowed her to go to the Gulf of California. Her goal there was to research the powerful six-foot-long Humboldt Squid. It was a time of personal discovery that gave Mayor the opportunity to climb rocky cliffs and look at untouched tropical ecosystems.

An expedition also led Mayor to Namibia. She went into a veterinarian's haven, or safe place, for leopards. "While caring for the leopards," Mayor explains, "the vet accidentally discovered a cure for fluid in the brain. It is a disease that also occurs in human infants. As a result of our film and the **media attention** it received, new studies are now taking place in children's hospitals. That is why I consider my television work just as important as my **conservation field work**," she notes. "The TV series **sheds light** on the plight of **endangered** species and animals around the world. Television has the power to help people know and connect with these animals and habitats that are disappearing. We may be facing the largest mass extinction of our time. Awareness is crucial. If we don't act now, it will be too late."

media attention positive news stories
conservation field work work to save species in the wild
sheds light focuses attention

▶ **Before You Continue**

1. **Fact/Opinion** What is one fact and one opinion that Mayor expresses?
2. **Explain** Why does Mayor consider her television work just as important as her conservation field work?

MIREYA MAYOR
EXPLORER/CORRESPONDENT

"I had to get that documentation because only then was I able to lobby to have its (the lemur's) habitat fully protected," said Mayor.

Mayor went to Madagascar on another of her National Geographic Explorer expeditions. On that expedition, she discovered a new species of lemurs. This discovery brought everyone's attention to Mayor's work. She had to document it. Once it was documented, she could try to obtain **protection** for the animal's habitat. This required grueling fieldwork during the **monsoon** season. "There we were, tromping through remote areas of jungle, rain pouring, tents blowing. We were looking for **a nocturnal animal**. One that happens to be the smallest primate in the world," she says. Her careful research and documentation were important. She was able to convince Madagascar's president to declare the species' habitat a national park. Soon after that, the president also agreed to triple the number of protected areas in the nation. As Mayor reports, one tiny discovery became "a **huge ambassador** for **all things wild** in Madagascar."

Mayor believes that local support for conservation is a key **factor** in bringing about change. "The local people are at the **very core** of **effective** conservation. Without their support, the 'dream' of saving the planet can never become a reality. The rainforest is literally their backyard. Yet many Malagasy kids have

monsoon rainy
a nocturnal animal an animal that is active at night
huge ambassador popular representative
all things wild wildlife
very core most important part

Emerging Explorers
National Geographic's Next Generation

OUR EXPLORERS | ABOUT THE PROGRAM

MIREYA MAYOR
EXPLORER/CORRESPONDENT

NEWS

» Emerging Explorers News

» Photo Gallery: Best Mountain Photographs of the Year

» What Triggers Tornadoes? New Season May Hold Answers

AFRICA

MADAGASCAR

never even seen a lemur. So I organize lots of field trips into the forest. Only by seeing how amazing these creatures are, will kids want to protect them." Mayor stresses the importance of providing education and opportunities for local communities to learn about the threats to animals and how they can help. She believes it will be critical to protecting the planet.

Mayor **circles the globe** on television expeditions, but her heart remains in the rainforests of Madagascar. As she describes it, "This phenomenal natural laboratory could vanish in our lifetime. It could become the stuff of history books, not science books. Until I can walk away . . . and know it's going to be okay, I just can't leave. ❖

Healthy Rainforest

Destroyed Rainforest

▲ Mayor's conservation work makes locals aware that the destruction of the rainforest threatens the lives of plants and animals.

circles the globe travels around the world

▶ **Before You Continue**

1. **Cause/Effect** Name two things Madagascar's president changed as a result of Mayor's work.

2. **Author's Viewpoint** How does the author show how much Mayor cares about her work?

Compare Authors' Viewpoints

Both "A Natural Balance" and "Mireya Mayor" describe the effects that people's activities have on the environment. Work with a partner to complete a Venn diagram that compares the authors' viewpoints. Then put together the details you recorded in the "Both" section to make a generalization, or statement, that is true for both authors.

Venn Diagram

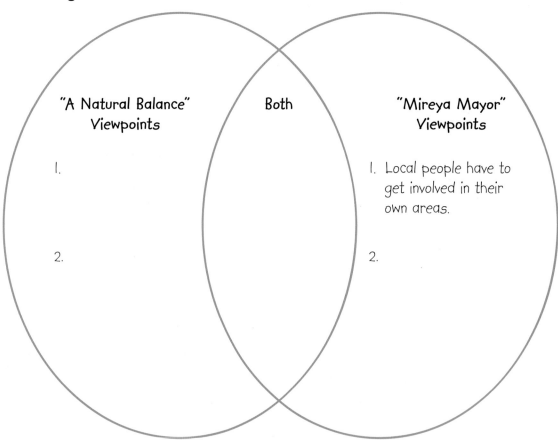

"A Natural Balance" Viewpoints

1.

2.

Both

"Mireya Mayor" Viewpoints

1. Local people have to get involved in their own areas.

2.

Talk Together

How do both texts address the value of diversity and balance in nature? How do they suggest that we should **sustain** a natural balance on Earth? Use **Key Words** and evidence from the text to talk about your ideas with a small group.

Adjectives and Adverbs

You can use **adjectives** and **adverbs** to describe and compare.

Grammar Rules Adjectives and Adverbs

There are similar rules for using **adjectives** and **adverbs** to compare.

	Adjective	Adverb
• To compare two nouns or actions, add **–er**. • For words with three or more syllables, use **more** or **less**.	**small<u>er</u>** <u>more</u> <u>incredible</u> <u>less</u> <u>threatening</u>	**fast<u>er</u>** <u>more</u> <u>rapidly</u> <u>less</u> <u>seriously</u>
• To compare three or more nouns or actions, add **–est**. • For words with three or more syllables, use **most** or **least**.	**small<u>est</u>** <u>most</u> <u>incredible</u> <u>least</u> <u>threatening</u>	**fast<u>est</u>** <u>most</u> <u>rapidly</u> <u>least</u> <u>seriously</u>
Some words have special forms for comparing.	<u>good</u> **better** best <u>bad</u> worse worst <u>many</u> more most	<u>well</u> better best <u>badly</u> worse worst

Read Adjectives and Adverbs

Good writers use adjectives and adverbs to make their writing more precise. Read these sentences from "A Natural Balance." What adjectives and adverbs can you find?

> • Better field research techniques give us faster and better data about endangered species.
>
> • There are many disagreements . . . about how best to take care of endangered species.

Write Adjectives and Adverbs

Write a paragraph that explains why we must help endangered species. Include adjectives and adverbs. Then compare your sentences with a partner's.

Formal Language	Informal Language
• Thank you for _____ .	• Thanks!
• May I _____ ?	• Let's _____ .
• Would you mind _____ ?	• Can you _____ ?

Use Appropriate Language

Listen to the discussions about a proposed hotel development on a beach. Then use **Language Frames** and appropriate language to talk about another environmental issue.

Save Our Beach 🔊

Thank you, City Council members, for allowing me to speak to you this evening. I am here to present objections to the proposed Mega-Hotel on Marsh Beach.

Look on the easel. The left side shows the beach as it is now. The right side shows what the beach would look like with the hotel.

Dude, that hotel would really wreck the beach!

Yeah, we sure couldn't surf there anymore.

Key Words

deforestation

ecological

landscape

management

regulate

Key Words

Look at these photographs and read the captions. Use **Key Words** and other words to talk about forests in the western United States.

▼ For many years, **deforestation** caused **ecological** damage to trees. Entire forests disappeared due to logging and natural fires. Without the trees, many animals and plants suffered.

▲ Today, many of the **landscapes** along the western coast of the U.S. include protected forests that everyone can enjoy.

◀ Since then, many groups have worked with the government to **regulate**, or control, how trees are used and replanted. This kind of careful **management** could help save many forests.

Talk Together

Pretend you are talking to teachers in your school about protecting natural habitats like forests or beaches. Use **Language Frames** from page 252 and **Key Words**. Be sure to use appropriate language for your audience.

253

Characters' Viewpoints

All people have viewpoints about the world and their own experiences. Characters in stories often have viewpoints, too. As you read, try to determine a character's viewpoint by analyzing the character's dialogue, thoughts, and actions.

Look Into the Text

His mom didn't answer, so Kale went looking for her. He and Noah found her in the kitchen. She was reading a letter—and frowning.

Kale dropped his book bag onto the table. "What's that?" he said.

His mom sighed. "The managers of our apartment complex think it's good news. I don't think you and Noah will agree with them."

"Kale's mom's **actions** show that she is worried."

"Kale's mom's **words** show that she has bad news for Kale and Noah."

Map and Talk

A character description chart can help you keep track of characters and their viewpoints based on evidence from the text.

Character Description Chart

Character	Evidence	Character's Viewpoint
Mom	• "The managers of our apartment complex think it's good news. I don't think you and Noah will agree with them."	• Mom does not agree with the management.

Talk Together

Tell a partner a story about two friends. Include details about what the characters say, think, and do. Have your partner use the information to create a character description chart for one of the characters in your story.

🔊 More Key Words

Use these words to talk about "If Trees Could Talk" and "The Super Trees."

advocate
verb

When you **advocate** something, you support it with words or actions. The dentist **advocates** brushing your teeth twice a day.

intervene
verb

When you **intervene**, you do something to change an event or a result. She **intervenes** when her sons argue.

obligation
noun

An **obligation** is something you must do. It is the boy's **obligation** to take care of the dog.

participate
verb

When you **participate**, you do something with others. These students **participate** on a sports team.

utilize
verb

When you **utilize** something, you use it to do a job. The gardeners **utilize** a shovel to collect leaves.

Talk Together

Make a Vocabulary Example Chart that includes each **Key Word**. Then compare your chart with a partner's.

Word	Definition/Synonym	Example
utilize	use	a pencil to write

Learn to Make Connections

As you read, make connections between what you already know about a topic and what you read about it. Connecting the text to what you know can help you add to your understanding of the text.

How to Make Connections

1. **Identify the Topic** As you read, figure out the topic—what the selection is mostly about.

2. **Look for Connections** As you read, pay attention to what you already know about the topic.

3. **Build Understanding** Connect what you read with what you know. Then explain how the connection helps you understand the text.

The topic is _____.

I already know _____.

Because I know _____, I understand _____.

Here's how one student made a connection to the text.

Look Into the Text

Dear Hawaiian Gardens Residents:

Good news! You asked for a new fitness center. We listened to your voices.

We'll begin **building a larger fitness center where the apartment complex's park now stands.** It's sad saying goodbye to our park, but the new center will allow more residents to participate in recreational activities.

"The topic is losing a green area. **I read** about the plans for Hawaiian Gardens. I already know that people care a lot about green areas. Now I understand why someone might not like these plans."

Making connections to what you're reading makes the text more interesting and easier to understand.

Talk Together

Read the blog post and sample notes. Use **Language Frames** to make connections as you read. Then talk with a partner about how your connections helped you understand the text.

Language Frames

The topic is _____.

I already know _____.

Because I know _____,
I understand _____.

Blog

Trina's Travels and Research

https://eltngl.com/reachhigherseries

Trina's Travels

| Blog | About Trina | Past Posts |

The Magic of Sandalwood
Tuesday, March 11 | **Author:** Trina

On my last trip, I visited Hawaii. I was amazed at the lush **landscapes** all around that included sandalwood trees. I became curious about this tree, since whenever I hear the word "sandalwood," a particular warm, sweet smell comes to my mind. I decided to find out more about this interesting tree. ◀

A sandalwood tree can grow to be 10 meters tall and has strong, leathery leaves. It takes a tree about 30 years to mature fully. Its true value is in the trunk and roots which contain a yellow oil that is used in fragrant products, such as soap or incense, as well as in medicine. The wood from the tree can be **utilized** for decorative objects and pieces of furniture. Such pieces will be durable and retain the extraordinary fragrance for years.

Its many uses and its unique smell make sandalwood desirable. I was sad to learn that in Hawaii, large forests were overexploited to extract the wood. **Deforestation** and the ensuing endangerment of the sandalwood tree in the islands followed. However, more than one **ecological** group has **intervened** to preserve native species of plants and animals on the islands. ◀

Authorities all over the world are recognizing that it is our **obligation** to preserve ecosystems. The responsible **management** of forests and green areas can result in sustainable use of important natural resources, such as the sandalwood tree, which is why different groups today **advocate** for laws that strictly **regulate** the harvesting of sandalwood in Hawaii. ◀

The topic is the sandalwood tree.

I already know that sandalwood has a pleasant smell.

Because I know that in Hawaii a lot of sandalwood trees were cut down to extract the wood, I understand that it is our obligation to preserve them.

◀ = a good place to stop and make a connection

Read Realistic Fiction

Genre

Realistic fiction is a story that seems as if it could be true. The characters, plot, and setting all seem real.

Writing Forms

Authors can use many different writing forms in fiction. Some writers show interaction between characters through a narrator's descriptions or characters' dialogue. Other writers may tell their stories in the forms of letters or journals. In this story, the characters write **letters** and post **signs** that include a mixture of formal and informal language.

Dear Hawaiian Gardens Residents:

Good news! You asked for a new fitness center. We listened to your voices.

formal language greeting

informal language in body of letter

IF TREES COULD TALK

by Lisa Harkrader

▶ **Set a Purpose**
Find out how the characters in the
story plan to save the park.

"Mom?" Kale **tromped** through the front door of his apartment, with his best friend, Noah, **on his heels**. "Noah and I are headed over to the park to play soccer."

His mom didn't answer, so Kale went looking for her. He and Noah found her in the kitchen. She was reading a letter—and frowning.

Kale dropped his book bag onto the table. "What's that?" he said.

His mom sighed. "The managers of our **apartment complex** think it's good news. I don't think you and Noah will agree with them."

She handed the letter to Kale. He began reading. Noah read over his shoulder.

tromped walked with heavy steps
on his heels behind him
apartment complex series of connected
buildings where people live

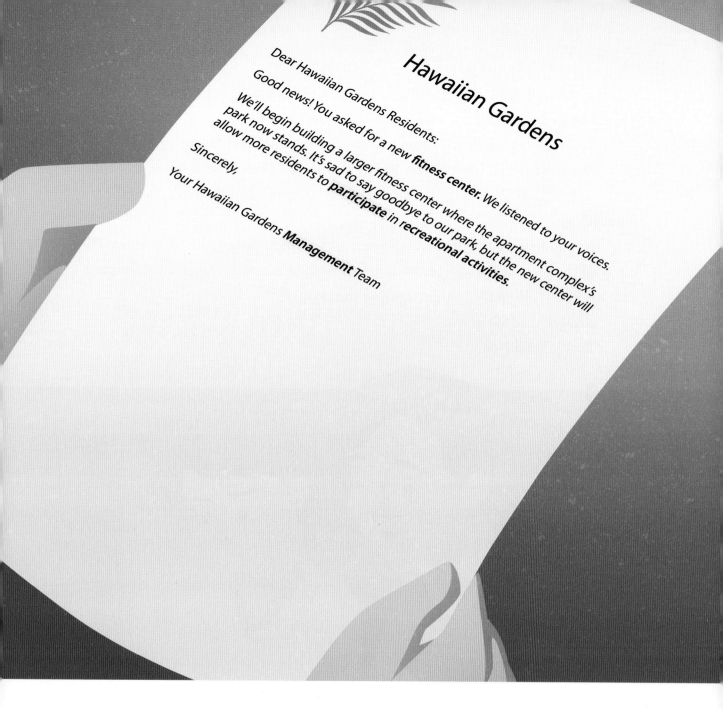

Hawaiian Gardens

Dear Hawaiian Gardens Residents:

Good news! You asked for a new **fitness center.** We listened to your voices.

We'll begin building a larger fitness center where the apartment complex's park now stands. It's sad to say goodbye to our park, but the new center will allow more residents to **participate** in **recreational activities.**

Sincerely,

Your Hawaiian Gardens **Management** Team

Noah shook his head. "That's not good news at all."

"Voices?" said Kale. "Whose voices did they listen to?"

"Not ours," said Noah. "We're losing our park."

"Maybe they should hear *your* voices," said Kale's mom.

Kale stared at the letter. "Maybe they should."

fitness center indoor space where people exercise
recreational activities sports and hobbies done for
    enjoyment

Noah swallowed. "We're going to talk to the apartment managers?"

"We are," said Kale.

"You really think they'll listen to a couple of kids?" said Noah.

"Not if we sound like **clueless kids**," said Kale. "*They* wrote a letter, so *we'll* write a letter back. We'll organize our thoughts on paper and then take it to the management office."

Kale **booted up** the family computer, and he and Noah wrote their letter. They listed all the reasons the apartment complex needed the park. When they finished, Kale hit PRINT. He pulled the letter from the printer.

"Ready?" said Kale.

"Ready," said Noah.

clueless kids young people who don't know a lot

booted up turned on

Kale and Noah **trotted** from Kale's building to the Hawaiian Gardens **management** office. The two assistant managers looked up as Kale and Noah **shuffled in**.

Miss Russell smiled. "Kale. Noah. Nice to see you."

"Can we help you?" asked Mr. James.

Kale cleared his throat. "We're here to let the management team hear our voices," he said, the way he'd practiced.

"O-kaaay." Miss Russell frowned, but she led them into the office of the manager, Ms. Alana. Mr. James followed.

Kale held the letter up so he and Noah could take turns reading it. His hands shook, but he began speaking.

trotted ran
shuffled in entered nervously

▶ **Before You Continue**

1. **Character's Viewpoint** What evidence shows how Kale and Noah feel about the new fitness center?

2. **Make Connections** How does your experience of being Kale and Noah's age help you understand the characters' problem?

263

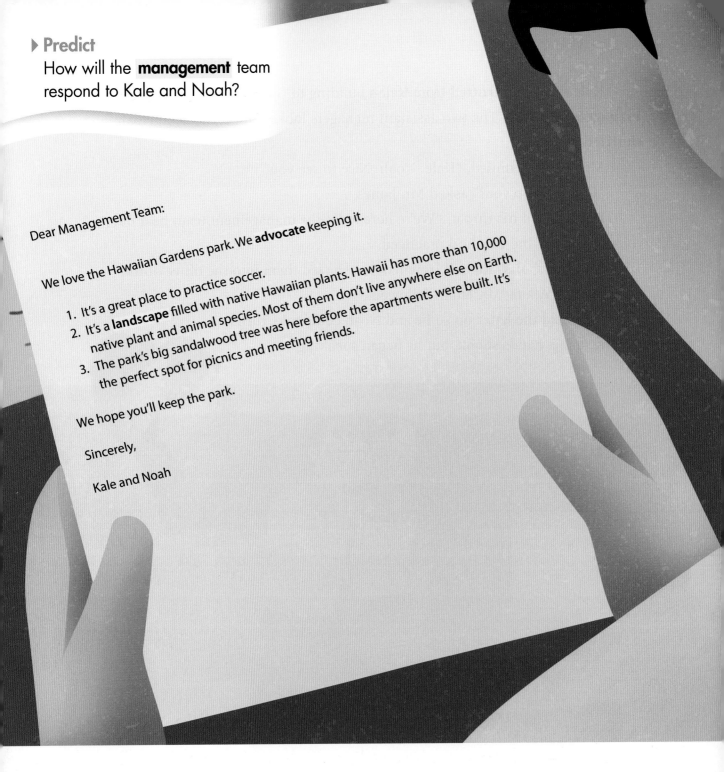

Dear Management Team:

We love the Hawaiian Gardens park. We **advocate** keeping it.

1. It's a great place to practice soccer.
2. It's a **landscape** filled with native Hawaiian plants. Hawaii has more than 10,000 native plant and animal species. Most of them don't live anywhere else on Earth.
3. The park's big sandalwood tree was here before the apartments were built. It's the perfect spot for picnics and meeting friends.

We hope you'll keep the park.

Sincerely,

Kale and Noah

They finished reading. Ms. Alana smiled. It was the smile adults use when they think kids are cute but not serious.

"Thank you," said Ms. Alana. "But we have an **obligation** to keep Hawaiian Gardens enjoyable for residents. We think more people will **utilize** the fitness center than the park."

"So . . . that's it?" said Kale. "No park?"

Ms. Alana nodded. "We've made our decision."

Miss Russell walked Kale and Noah out. "Ten thousand native species? Really?"

Noah nodded. "We learned about them in school."

"Then we found some of them in the Hawaiian Gardens park," said Kale.

Future Home of
Hawaiian Gardens
Fitness Center

He and Noah left the office and trudged across the apartment complex. When they reached the park, Kale stopped. He stared at the big sandalwood tree.

A large sign announcing the fitness center had been pounded in the ground in front of the tree.

"That was fast," said Noah.

Kale nodded. "No wonder they didn't listen to us."

"They probably wouldn't listen to anybody, not even . . . not even"—Noah flung a hand toward the sandalwood—"this tree."

"This tree." Kale blinked. "You're a genius. We'll give the *tree* a voice."

Noah frowned. "We're going to get a tree to talk?"

"We are," said Kale.

Kale raced to his apartment, with Noah on his heels. They found a piece of cardboard and made their own sign.

Kale and Noah returned to the park. They hung their sign on the sandalwood. They stepped back to admire their work.

I'm a sandalwood tree. My species of sandalwood is native to Hawaii. I don't grow anywhere else in the world. Because of **deforestation**, sandalwood trees **were nearly wiped out** on the Hawaiian islands. But we've started to **make a comeback**. Please don't cut me down.

"You think it'll do any good?" said Noah.

Kale shook his head. "Probably not. It sounds like the managers' **minds are made up**. But at least they'll see there are other voices worth hearing."

were nearly wiped out almost disappeared
make a comeback return
minds are made up decision has been made

When Kale and Noah passed the park after school the next day, they stopped short.

"**Whoa!**" said Noah.

Kale nodded. Someone—or several someones—had placed more signs on the sandalwood tree.

> As a plant, I have **ecological** benefits. I **absorb** carbon dioxide and pollution and give off oxygen. A big tree like me can provide enough oxygen in a day for four people.

> I **regulate** temperature, kind of like a living air conditioner. My shade cools the area, including the nearby apartment buildings.

A few other residents were looking at the signs. Mr. James, the assistant manager, was with them.

"Whoa!" "Stop and look!"
absorb take in

As a plant, I have **ecological** benefits. I **absorb** carbon dioxide and pollution and give off oxygen. A big tree like me can provide enough oxygen in a day for four people.

I **regulate** temperature, kind of like a living air conditioner. My shade cools the area, including the nearby apartment buildings.

Future Home of Hawaiian Gardens Fitness Center

Half of the world's medicines were first discovered in plants. These medicines treat problems such as heart disease, cancer, infections, and pain. What if we destroy a plant that might contain the cure to a serious disease?

Mr. James was reading a sign someone had taped to the "Future Home of Hawaiian Gardens Fitness Center" sign.

> Half of the world's medicines were first discovered in plants. These medicines treat problems such as heart disease, cancer, infections, and pain. What if we destroy a plant that might contain the cure to a serious disease?

"My grandmother takes medicine for her heart," he said. "I wonder if it came from a plant."

Mr. James rubbed his chin and **stared** at the sign, and then he headed back to the apartment **management** office.

"I think that sign **spoke to him**," said Noah.

stared looked hard
spoke to him made him think

▶ **Before You Continue**

1. **Character's Viewpoint** What influences Mr. James's views about the importance of the park? Give examples from the text.

2. **Make Connections** How do your own experiences help you better understand the characters?

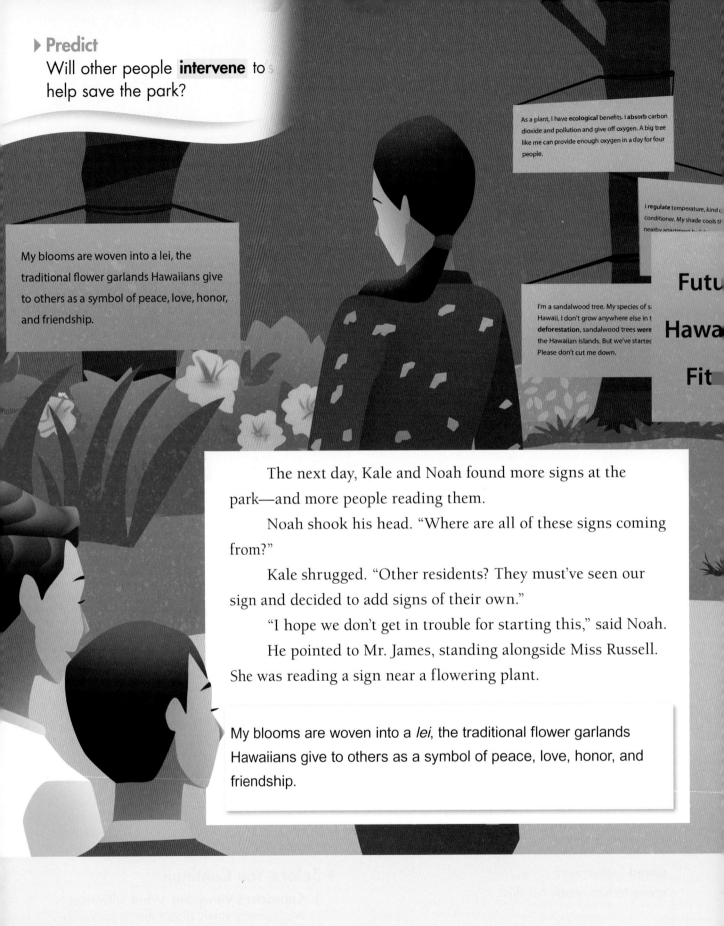

▶ **Predict**
Will other people **intervene** to ...
help save the park?

As a plant, I have **ecological** benefits. I absorb carbon dioxide and pollution and give off oxygen. A big tree like me can provide enough oxygen in a day for four people.

I **regulate** temperature, kind o...
conditioner. My shade cools th...
nearby apartment b...

My blooms are woven into a lei, the traditional flower garlands Hawaiians give to others as a symbol of peace, love, honor, and friendship.

I'm a sandalwood tree. My species of s...
Hawaii. I don't grow anywhere else in t
deforestation, sandalwood trees were
the Hawaiian islands. But we've started
Please don't cut me down.

Futu

Hawa

Fit

The next day, Kale and Noah found more signs at the park—and more people reading them.

Noah shook his head. "Where are all of these signs coming from?"

Kale shrugged. "Other residents? They must've seen our sign and decided to add signs of their own."

"I hope we don't get in trouble for starting this," said Noah.

He pointed to Mr. James, standing alongside Miss Russell. She was reading a sign near a flowering plant.

My blooms are woven into a *lei*, the traditional flower garlands Hawaiians give to others as a symbol of peace, love, honor, and friendship.

I prevent **erosion**. Without plants, rainwater would wash away soil and rocks, causing landslides and pushing **sediment** to the ocean, damaging our beaches and **coral reefs**.

Half of the world's medicines were firs discovered in pla These medicir problems suc disease, canc infections, ar What if we d plant that m the cure to ; disease?

ne of

rdens

ter

Kale and Noah nervously watched Miss Russell and Mr. James. Miss Russell studied the flower sign thoughtfully and then moved toward another sign, this one on the sandalwood tree.

I prevent **erosion**. Without plants, rainwater would wash away soil and rocks, causing landslides and pushing **sediment** to the ocean, damaging our beaches and **coral reefs**.

She shook her head. "I love the beach," she said. "I love to **surf**. I love to **snorkel** around the coral reefs."

Noah looked at Kale. "You were right. You said we should give plants a voice."

Kale nodded. "They're speaking louder than I ever thought."

erosion the slow wearing away of part of nature
sediment small bits of rock and dirt
coral reefs long rock-like structures in the sea where
many species live
surf ride on ocean waves
snorkel swim underwater while breathing through
a tube

"Maybe *too* loud," said Noah.

He nudged Kale, and they both turned to see Ms. Alana striding toward the park.

"I don't think she's going to be happy about this," said Kale.

Ms. Alana stopped in front of the sandalwood tree, hands on her hips. She scrutinized one sign and then another. Then she looked up and saw Kale and Noah.

"Are you two responsible for this?" Ms. Alana waved a hand toward all the signs in the park.

"Um, yes." Kale swallowed. "I mean, maybe. We put up the first sign."

"And then all these other signs just appeared," said Noah.

"I'm glad you **intervened**," said Ms. Alana.

Kale blinked. "You are?"

Ms. Alana pointed to a sign Kale hadn't noticed before.

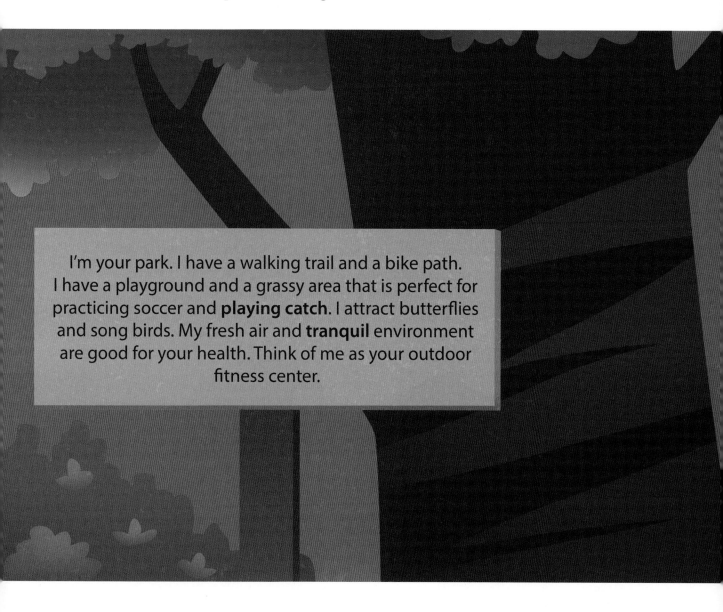

I'm your park. I have a walking trail and a bike path. I have a playground and a grassy area that is perfect for practicing soccer and **playing catch**. I attract butterflies and song birds. My fresh air and **tranquil** environment are good for your health. Think of me as your outdoor fitness center.

"You and the signs and the park itself have given me an idea," said Ms. Alana.

Kale nodded. He hoped her idea was a good one.

playing catch throwing a ball back and forth
tranquil peaceful; quiet

The next day, Kale tromped into his apartment, with Noah on his heels. He found his mom in the kitchen, reading a letter.

Kale stopped. "Is that—?"

"From the apartment managers?" his mom nodded.

She handed the letter to Kale and Noah.

Dear Hawaiian Gardens Residents:

Good news! You asked for a new fitness center. We listened to your voices—*all* your voices.

Instead of building a new center, we'll **upgrade** our existing center and also offer exercise classes in our park. This way, you'll be able to enjoy two fitness centers—one indoors and one outdoors.

Sincerely,

Your Hawaiian Gardens Management Team ❖

upgrade make improvements to

▶ **Before You Continue**

1. **Character** Ms. Alana agrees to save the park. What does this tell you about her?

2. **Make Comparisons** Use text evidence to compare residents' opinions about the park at the beginning of the story and at the end. What changed their minds?

Meet the Author

Lisa Harkrader

When she was growing up, Lisa Harkrader's greatest love was reading. Stories and books took her to places and into lives she could never know without reading. She believes stories are an important way for readers to understand and develop empathy for people, places, and problems that are much different from their own. Harkrader has passion for protecting endangered animals, plants, and habitats. She chose Hawaii as the setting for "If Trees Could Talk" to bring attention to the many endangered species on the islands.

Harkrader believes that reading is also an important part of being a writer. Her love of books made her realize that she wanted to more than simply read stories. She wanted to write them, too. Perhaps one of her stories will inspire readers to write about what they love, too.

Writing Tip

In "If Trees Could Talk," the characters use letters to write about issues they feel strongly about. Write your own letter to a friend. Use informal language and specific details to write about an issue that is important to you.

Key Words

advocate	management
deforestation	obligation
ecological	participate
intervene	regulate
landscape	utilize

Talk About It 💬

1. What makes the characters in the story seem realistic? Use text evidence to support your answer.

2. The author uses letters to tell part of the story. How do the letters help you understand the point of view of the **management** team?

3. The author uses dialogue to tell part of the story. How does the dialogue help you understand each character?

4. Imagine you are Kale. Use appropriate language to speak to the residents of Hawaiian Gardens about saving the park.

5. How do Kale and Noah feel when they see the signs they did not write? Use text evidence to determine their viewpoint.

6. Based on what you have read, what can you infer about Ms. Alana and her viewpoint about **deforestation** and the management of the Hawaiian Gardens community? Cite text evidence to support your answer.

Write About It ✏

Based on what you know about the Hawaiian Gardens management team, how do you think Ms. Alana might have responded to Kale and Noah's letter of appeal? Write a response letter from Ms. Alana to Kale and Noah. Use at least three **Key Words** and appropriate language as you write from Ms. Alana's viewpoint.

> Dear Kale and Noah,
>
> I'm sorry you are so upset about the proposed project in our park. Deforestation is difficult for many people, but the management team needs to listen to residents who find the existing fitness center too small for the community's needs.

Characters' Viewpoints

Use the character description chart to record the dialogue, thoughts, and actions of the characters in "If Trees Could Talk." You can add as many details as needed to show the characters' viewpoints.

Character Description Chart

Character	Evidence	Character's Viewpoint
Noah	• Noah shook his head. "That's not good news at all." •	• Noah does not like the news about the park. •
Kale	• •	• •
Ms. Alana	• •	• •

Use your character description chart to explain each character's viewpoints to a partner. Use **Key Words**.

Fluency

Practice reading with expression. Rate your reading.

Talk Together

Consider the viewpoints of the characters in "If Trees Could Talk." Do they feel that diversity in nature is valuable? Discuss your ideas with a partner. Use **Key Words** and evidence from the text in your discussion.

Word Work

Greek and Latin Roots

Greek and Latin roots can make up English words. A root is a central word part that has meaning, but it is not a complete word. If you know the meanings of word parts like roots, prefixes, and suffixes, you can figure out the meaning of the word.

EXAMPLE

root meaning "together"		root meaning "to protect"		word meaning "to protect together"
con-	+	serv	=	conserve

Root	Orgin	Meaning	Example
eco	Greek	home (environment)	economy
log/logy	Greek	thought, study	ecology
ven/vent	Latin	come	intervene

The chart above shows more Greek and Latin roots and their definitions. The Latin root *ad* means "towards," and the root *voc* means "to call or speak." What do you think *advocate* means?

Try It

Read the sentences. Then answer the questions. Use the chart to help you.

Kale and Noah want to <u>intervene</u> to stop the management team from building in the park area. <u>Ecology</u> is important to them because they understand the benefits of green areas.

1. **The prefix *inter-* means "between." What is the best meaning for intervene?**

   A come again

   B come between

   C stop from coming

   D come toward

2. **What is the best meaning for the word ecology in the sentence?**

   A study of the environment

   B harm to the environment

   C saving the environment

   D in the environment

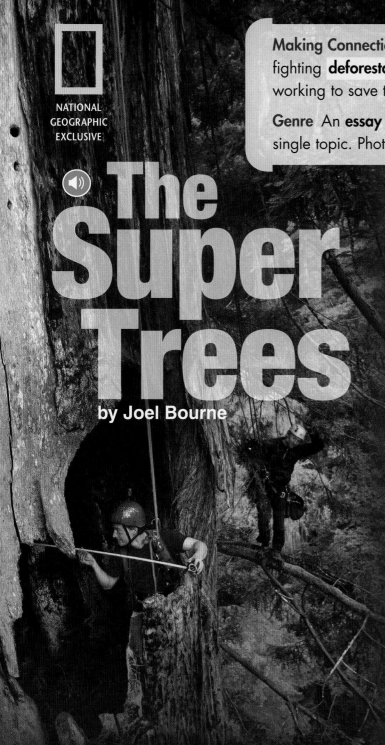

NATIONAL GEOGRAPHIC EXCLUSIVE

Making Connections You read about fictional characters fighting **deforestation**. Now learn how real scientists are working to save the forests.

Genre An **essay** is a short nonfiction text that explores a single topic. Photos often provide information about the topic.

The Super Trees

by Joel Bourne

Scientists investigate a hole in a redwood tree that was caused by a forest fire. This tree has been burned in two fires, but it is still standing.

John Muir was one of the first people to **advocate** for protecting California's forests. In 1895, Muir gave a speech to the Sierra Club about the importance of national parks and protection for great trees like the redwoods and sequoias.

"The battle we have fought, and are still fighting, for the forests is a part of the eternal conflict between right and wrong, and we cannot expect to see the end of it. I trust, however, that [we] will not weary in this forest well-doing. The fight for the Yosemite Park and other forest parks and **reserves** *is* **by no means** *over; nor would the fighting cease, however much the boundaries were* **contracted**. *Every good thing, great and small, needs defense. . . . So we must count on watching and* **striving** *for these trees, and should always be glad to find anything so surely good and noble to strive for."* – John Muir

reserves *protected places*
by no means *not*
contracted *changed*
striving *fighting*

▶ **Before You Continue**

1. **Paraphrase** In your own words, explain John Muir's viewpoint about protecting forests.

2. **Make Connections** Consider what you know about trees, and read the caption. Why is the tree in this photo unique?

Now, more than 100 years later, John Muir's work to save the redwoods is carried on by people like Mike Fay. It could be said that the history of modern America is carved in redwood. Mike Fay has spent three decades helping save African forests. He is a Wildlife Conservation Society biologist and National Geographic Society explorer-in-residence.

Mike Fay's love for the **iconic** American trees began a few years ago after he explored the largest intact jungle remaining in Africa. One day while driving along the northern California coast, he found himself gazing at areas of clear-cuts and spindly **second-growth forests**. Another time in a state park, a six-foot-tall slice of an old redwood log on display caught his attention. Near the burgundy center a label read: "1492 Columbus."

"The one that **got me** was about three inches from the edge," Fay says. "'Gold Rush, 1849.' And I realized that within the last few inches of that tree's life, we'd very nearly **liquidated** a 2,000-year-old forest."

Mike Fay

◀ **By studying the rings formed within trees, scientists are able to estimate the ages of trees.**

iconic famous
second-growth forests forests that had been replanted and were growing back

got me made me feel strong emotions
liquidated destroyed

This **landscape** shows clear-cuts in a stand of spruce, fir, and redwood trees.

In the fall of 2007, he **resolved** to see for himself how Earth's tallest forest had been **exploited** in the past and how it is being treated today. He wanted to find out if there was a way to maximize both timber production and the many **ecological** and social benefits that forests provide. Fay started walking at the southern end of the forest. There the trees grow in scattered groves in the Santa Lucia Range and the Santa Cruz Mountains. In small parks like Muir Woods outside San Francisco and Big Basin near Santa Cruz, he encountered a few rare patches of ancient trees. He walked 1,800 miles through forests that had been cut at least once. Many had been cut three times since 1850. This left islands of larger second-growth forest in a sea of mostly small trees.

While Mike was walking, he saw many beautiful sights. Redwoods the size of Saturn rockets sprouted from the ground like giant beanstalks. The trees' trunks were blackened by fire. Some trees had thick, ropy bark that spiraled skyward in candy-cane swirls. Others had huge cavities big enough to hold 20 people. Treetops had plummeted from 30 stories up and were half-buried among the sorrel and sword ferns. They were the **casualties** of powerful wars with the wind, which even now coursed through the tops with creaks and groans.

resolved decided
exploited used
casualties victims

▶ **Before You Continue**

1. **Make Comparisons** How is the information from the photo and caption above different from the text about clear-cut forests?

2. **Explain** How does Mike Fay hope to save the redwoods? Use evidence from the text to support your response.

It was a good year to be walking the redwoods. The Pacific Lumber Company was bankrupt. It had spent more than two decades battling environmentalists and state and federal regulators over its aggressive cutting practices. Most of the remaining **old growth was** protected. However, the **emblematic** species of the great forests continued to lose numbers. Some of them included the northern spotted owls, elusive little seabirds called marbled murrelets, and coho salmon.

Something else was **taking root among** the trees. Environmental groups, consulting foresters, and even a few timber companies and communities agreed that the redwoods were at a historic crossroads. It was a time when society could move beyond the log/don't log debates of decades past. They could embrace a different kind of forestry that could benefit people, wildlife, and perhaps even the planet.

The **mantra** of industrial foresters has long been to grow trees as fast as possible to maximize the return on investment. This method provided a steady flow of wood products to market. Now foresters are changing to a form of single-tree selection. This is more productive in the long run than clear-cutting. Every 10 to 15 years they take about a third of the timber in a stand. They only cut down the least robust trees. This creates more open space and allows the remaining trees to get a greater share of sunlight. This also speeds their growth. Every year, the amount and quality of the standing wood increase. The process can proceed for centuries. The advantages are two-fold: short-term income and a larger payback over the long term.

This change isn't just about wood. Past damage to ecosystems is being repaired. Sediment is being excavated from streams to restore their flow. Trees identified as crucial for wildlife habitat are being preserved.

Mike Fay says, "This isn't about loving big trees. It's about the fact that I spent 333 days walking 1,800 miles through the entire range of the redwoods with a notebook in my hand, documenting details about this ecosystem—and witnessing the aftermath of the cutting of at least 95 percent of the most wood-laden forest on Earth. If you want clean water, salmon, wildlife, and high-quality lumber, you've got to have a forest.

old growth was old forests were
emblematic important
taking root among starting because of
mantra belief

A black bear walks through a redwood forest.

"With increased production for humanity also come healthy ecosystems and global balance. We can—and must—do this not just with our forests and wildlife but also with the fish in our oceans and streams, the soils on our farms, and the grass in our pastures. The redwoods can show us the way." ❖

▶ **Before You Continue**

1. **Author's Purpose** Why does the author end this essay about redwoods with Mike Fay's viewpoint about "global balance"?

2. **Make Connections** What parts of this essay connect to other **ecological** problems you know?

Respond and Extend

Key Words

advocate	obligation
deforestation	management
ecological	participate
intervene	regulate
landscape	utilize

Compare Genres

"If Trees Could Talk" and "The Super Trees" both focus on
the importance of trees and green areas. Use a comparison chart
to show how the selections are similar and different. Then use the
comparison to help draw a conclusion that is true for both selections.

Comparison Chart

	"If Trees Could Talk"	**"The Super Trees"**
Genre		
Main Characters or People		biologist and explorer Mike Fay
Text Features and Forms	informal dialogue letters and signs illustrations	
Important Events		
Author's or Character's Viewpoint		

Talk Together

Is diversity important? With a partner, discuss how each selection addresses this
question. Then use the conclusion you drew above to form a generalization about
diversity. Use **Key Words** and evidence from the text to talk about your ideas.

Participial Phrases

A **participle** is a verb form that often ends with **-ed** or **-ing**. It can be used alone or appear at the start of a group of words called a **participial phrase**.

Grammar Rules Participial Phrases

A **participle** or a **participial phrase** acts as an adjective to describe a **noun** or **pronoun**.	The **rustling trees** were huge. Mike had discovered **them growing** gracefully.
Insert a comma (**,**) after a **participle** or a **participial phrase** that begins a sentence.	**Walking** through the forest, **Mike** saw many trees.
Insert a comma (**,**) both before and after a **participle** or a **participial phrase** that identifies or explains the **noun** or **pronoun** that comes before it.	Now, the **trees, blackened by fire,** were dead.

Read Participial Phrases

Good writers often use participles and participial phrases to make their writing more interesting and descriptive. Read this passage based on "If Trees Could Talk." What participles and participial phrases can you find? What extra details do they add?

> Knowing we would not like the message, my mom handed us the letter and we read it. Confused by the bad news, we asked ourselves what could be done to save the park. My mom, noticing our concern, encouraged us to say something.

Write Participial Phrases

Reread page 268 of "If Trees Could Talk." Write a summary of the scene where Kale and Noah see more signs. Include at least one participle and two participial phrases in your sentences. Be sure to use commas correctly. Then compare your sentences with a partner's.

Write as an Advocate

Write an Argument ✎

How can you help endangered animals, plants, or trees? Write an argument that persuades people to find a way to help an endangered species. Post your argument on a blog or bulletin board entitled "Helping Endangered Species."

Study a Model

In an argument, you present your claim, or opinion. You use reasons and evidence to show why readers should agree with your claim and change what they think or do. Read Rafael's argument about helping an endangered species.

Help the California Condor
by Rafael Pincay

Rafael organizes his argument by introducing his **claim**.

Do you want to help endangered animals but don't know how? **You should join Condor Watch to help save the California condor.**

Condor Watch needs volunteers like you. According to the U.S. Fish and Wildlife Service, only about 200 California condors live in the wild. Scientists have installed remote-controlled cameras to take thousands of photos of condors. Volunteers collect data from the many photos. This data helps scientists understand condor behavior and threats to their survival.

In the following paragraphs, Rafael clearly organizes the **reasons** for his claim. He develops and supports the reasons with specific **evidence**.

Participating in Condor Watch is easy because all you need is online access. The website shows you how to identify condors in a photo and send the information to researchers. You can do real scientific research right from home.

The conclusion tells what **action** Rafael wants people to take.

Condor Watch is a great way to help save an animal. **Log on to join Condor Watch today and help save condors!**

Prewrite

1. **Choose a Topic** What argument could you make to persuade people to help an endangered plant or animal? Talk with a partner to find an idea.

Language Frames	
Tell Your Ideas	**Respond to Ideas**
• One thing I've learned about _____ is _____ . • One way to help an endangered species is _____ . • I'd like to persuade people to _____ .	• I'm not clear about your opinion about _____ . Can you clarify? • I'm not sure exactly what you want people to do about _____ . Can you tell me more? • I don't think I agree with your idea because _____ .

2. **Gather Information** What reasons will you give to support your claim? What evidence can you give to develop your reasons? Where can you locate credible sources for your reasons and evidence?

3. **Get Organized** Use a chart to help you organize your ideas.

Claim-and-Evidence Chart

Claim	Reasons and Evidence	Action Needed
Joining Condor Watch is a great way to help save California condors.	Condor Watch needs volunteers to collect data from photos of wild condors.	

Draft

Use your claim-and-evidence chart as you write your draft. Begin by stating your claim, or opinion about the topic. Support your claim with reasons and evidence. Then conclude by telling readers what action you want them to take.

Revise

1. **Read, Retell, Respond** Read your draft aloud to a partner. Your partner listens and then retells your main points. Then talk about ways to improve your writing.

Language Frames	
Retell	**Make Suggestions**
• Your claim is _____ .	• The relationship between your claim and reasons isn't clear. Could you add a transition, such as _____ ?
• The reasons and evidence you gave included _____ .	• Could you add more evidence to support _____ ?
• You want people to _____ .	• I'm not sure what you want people to do. Maybe you could _____ .

2. **Make Changes** Think about your draft and your partner's suggestions. Use revision marks to make your changes.

   • Make sure your evidence is specific and from a credible source.

   > According to the U.S. Fish and Wildlife Service, only about 200
   > ~~Only a few~~ ∧ California condors live in the wild.

   • Did you connect your claims, reasons, and evidence? Would adding transitions make the connections clearer?

   > Participating in Condor Watch is easy. ∧ All you need is
   > *because*
   > online access.

   • Make sure that your readers know what action to take.

   > Log on to join Condor Watch today and
   > ∧ Help save condors!

Punctuation Tip

Use punctuation, such as commas, parentheses, or dashes, to set off participial phrases.

Edit and Proofread

Work with a partner to edit and proofread your argument. Pay special attention to adjectives, adverbs, and participial phrases. Use revision marks to show your changes.

Present

1. **On Your Own** Make a final copy of your argument. Put the key points on note cards and present it to your class as a persuasive speech.

Presentation Tips	
If you are the speaker . . .	**If you are the listener . . .**
Be sure to make eye contact with listeners as you speak. Use appropriate language.	Do you understand all the speaker's reasons? If not, ask questions.
Clarify your ideas and answer listeners' questions or counterarguments with more reasons and evidence.	Evaluate whether the speaker has supported his or her claim with sufficient reasons and evidence.

2. **In a Group** Gather all the arguments from your class. Post them on a class blog or a bulletin board called "Helping Endangered Animals."

https://eltngl.com/reachhigherseries

Helping Endangered Animals

HOME   BLOG   LINKS

Help the California Condor
by Rafael Pincay

Do you want to help endangered animals but don't know how? You should join Condor Watch to help save the California condor.

Condor Watch needs volunteers like you. According to the U.S. Fish and Wildlife Service, only about 200 California condors live in the wild. Scientists have installed remote-controlled

BIG Question — Why is diversity important?

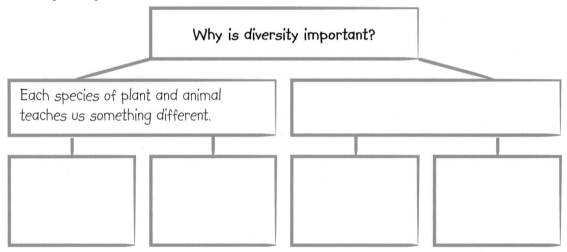

Talk Together

In this unit you found many answers to the **Big Question**. Now use your concept map to discuss it. Think about the different ideas presented in the selections. Why is diversity important and what we can do to protect our environment?

Concept Map

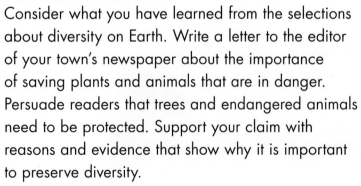

Why is diversity important?

Each species of plant and animal teaches us something different.

Performance Task: Argument

Consider what you have learned from the selections about diversity on Earth. Write a letter to the editor of your town's newspaper about the importance of saving plants and animals that are in danger. Persuade readers that trees and endangered animals need to be protected. Support your claim with reasons and evidence that show why it is important to preserve diversity.

Checklist

Does your letter to the editor

✔ use text evidence from the selections about saving plants and animals in danger?

✔ include relevant evidence to support your claim?

✔ include a concluding statement that clearly follows from and supports the claim?

Share Your Ideas

Choose one of these ways to share your ideas about the **Big Question**.

Write It!

Write a Speech

Research an animal that is endangered. Write a speech to persuade your classmates to save this animal. Back up your claim with reasons and evidence. Explain what actions students could take. Then present the speech to your class.

Talk About It!

Make a Presentation

Use the Internet to research redwood trees and why they are important to the environment. Use presentation software to include photos and text in your presentation.

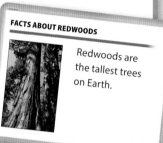

FACTS ABOUT REDWOODS

Redwoods are the tallest trees on Earth.

Do It!

Perform a Skit

Think about the selection "If Trees Could Talk." Perform a skit with a group of classmates about what might happen if Kale and Noah had to protect another green area in their neighborhood. What could they do to change a developer's decision to cut down trees to build a new shopping mall?

Write It!

Write a Short Story

Imagine that you are exploring Madagascar when you discover a new species. Write a short story about your expedition. What new species did you discover? Why is the discovery of this new species important? In your short story, describe why diversity is important to you and your research.

Dictionary

The definitions are for the words as they are introduced in the selections of this book.

Parts of an Entry

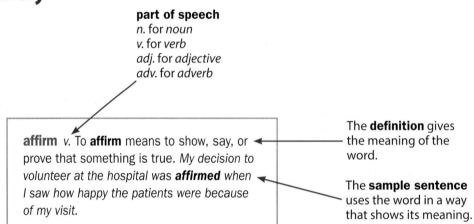

part of speech
n. for *noun*
v. for *verb*
adj. for *adjective*
adv. for *adverb*

affirm *v.* To **affirm** means to show, say, or prove that something is true. *My decision to volunteer at the hospital was affirmed when I saw how happy the patients were because of my visit.*

The **definition** gives the meaning of the word.

The **sample sentence** uses the word in a way that shows its meaning.

A

advocate *v.* When you **advocate** something, you support it with words or actions. *The dentist advocates brushing your teeth twice a day.*

analytical *adj.* When you study something in an **analytical** way, you break the information into parts so that it is easier to understand. *A scientist does an analytical study of the liquid by separating it and studying each part.*

appeal *n.* An **appeal** is a serious request for help. *The student made an appeal to his teacher for help with a project.*

archaeological *adj.* An **archaeological** expedition focuses on studying the remains of ancient civilizations in order to understand them. *He found a fragment of an ancient Egyptian jug on his first archaeological dig.*

artifact *n.* An **artifact** is an object, or the remains of one, created by humans during a certain period in history. *The jar was an artifact from Hatshepsut's reign.*

asset *n.* An **asset** is something valuable and useful. *When you are hiking, a compass is a helpful asset that shows direction.*

associate *v.* **Associate** means to keep company with someone. *She associated with the new girl in school when she ate lunch with her.*

assumption *n.* An **assumption** is something that is believed to be true. *When the dog wagged its tail, the boy made the assumption that the dog was friendly.*

awareness *n.* When you have **awareness** of something, you see or understand it. *They used their awareness of traffic and safety rules to cross the street.*

C

camouflage *n.* **Camouflage** is a color or pattern that helps people or animals hide. *People use camouflage to help them hide when they hunt.*

capable *adj.* To be **capable** means to be able to do something without any problems. *Because she studied, she was capable of passing her test.*

chamber *n.* A **chamber** is a special room. *The Egyptians had burial chambers filled with gold.*

chronological *adj.* When something is in **chronological** order, it is arranged in the order that the events happened. *Historians use a chronological timeline to chart the events in ancient Egypt.*

civilization *n.* A **civilization** is the culture of a specific place, time, or group of people. *Greece has a very old civilization.*

command *v.* To **command** is for someone in power to give an order. *The pharaoh commanded the people to build a new pyramid.*

concentrate *v.* When you **concentrate**, you give all of your attention to something. *He must concentrate when he glues the tiny pieces together.*

conform *v.* When you **conform**, you follow a rule or way of doing things. *In some schools, all students must conform to a dress code by wearing a uniform.*

confront *v.* To **confront** means to come face to face with something or someone. *He confronted his fear of public speaking when he gave the speech in front of the class.*

consider *v.* When you **consider** something, you think about it carefully. *The boy considers which snack to choose.*

contribute *v.* To **contribute** means to give something to others. *Each student will contribute one dollar to help people in need.*

convince *v.* To **convince** means to make someone believe something is true. *The kids will convince their mother to agree with their idea.*

D

deception *n.* **Deception** is the act of tricking something or someone. *The white moth on the white tree bark caused a visual deception so we could not see the moth.*

deforestation *n.* **Deforestation** is the act of cutting down forests. *Uncontrolled deforestation almost destroyed the redwoods.*

dependent *adj.* When you are **dependent** on something, you need it. *Babies are dependent on their parents for everything.*

depict *v.* When you **depict** something, you show it in a picture or with words. *The artist's drawing depicts the woman.*

diverge *v.* When two things or ideas **diverge**, they differ or move away from each other. *This hiking trail has two paths that diverge in different directions.*

duplicate *v.* To **duplicate** means to copy something. *The fish duplicated the movement of the plant and blended into the background.*

Dictionary

dynasty *n.* A **dynasty** is a sequence of rulers from the same family or group. *When Rome took over Egypt, Cleopatra's **dynasty** ended.*

E

ecological *adj.* When something is **ecological**, it means that it considers the relationship between organisms and their environments. *The new **ecological** plan to preserve the wetlands would save many animals.*

effective *adj.* Something that is **effective** has good results. *An umbrella is **effective** for keeping dry in the rain.*

emerge *v.* To **emerge** is to appear from somewhere hidden. *The sun will soon **emerge** from behind dark clouds.*

encounter *v.* To **encounter** something or someone is to experience something or meet someone unexpectedly. *We **encountered** some problems at the start of our science project.*

endangered *adj.* To be **endangered** means to be at risk of disappearing forever. *The ivory-billed woodpecker is an example of an **endangered** animal.*

ensure *v.* To **ensure** means to make certain. *This girl uses a watch to **ensure** that she meets her friend on time.*

exclude *v.* When you **exclude** something, you leave it out. *I **exclude** nuts from the recipe because I am allergic to them.*

exhaust *v.* To **exhaust** means to use up something. *He **exhausted** his supply of water, because his water bottle was empty.*

extinct *adj.* Something that is **extinct** is no longer living. *The dodo bird became **extinct** because people hunted too many over time.*

F

factor *n.* A **factor** is something that can lead to a specific result. *Heavy rains were a **factor** in the terrible flooding.*

figure out *v.* To **figure out** means to decide about something. *She **figured out** that if she saved her chore money, then she could go to the movies.*

H

hieroglyphics *n.* **Hieroglyophics** were a special form of writing used by the Egyptians. *__Hieroglyphics__ were written all over the walls in the Egyptian tombs.*

I

impact *n.* An **impact** is the effect one thing has on another. *The creative science teacher had a positive **impact** on her students.*

intense *adj.* Something that is **intense** is very strong. *The **intense** wind made the tree tops bend over.*

intent *n.* An **intent** is a plan to do something. *The student studies hard with the **intent** of passing a difficult test.*

interaction *n.* An **interaction** is when people talk or do activities with one another. *This is an **interaction** between three friends.*

intervene *v.* When you **intervene**, you do something to change an event or a result. *She **intervenes** when her sons argue.*

involve *v.* To **involve** means to include. *Winning a baseball game may **involve** speed, strength, and teamwork.*

L

landscape *n.* A **landscape** is an area of land that you can see. *She admired the **landscape** of the mountains in the distance.*

M

management *n.* **Management** is the conducting or supervising of something. *The lemonade stand was successful under her **management**.*

mimic *v.* **Mimic** means to imitate closely. *The mockingbird **mimics** the sounds of other birds.*

motivation *n.* **Motivation** is the reason for doing something. *My **motivation** for studying is to get good grades.*

N

necessity *n.* A **necessity** is an item that someone needs. *Food and water are the most basic necessities of life.*

O

obligation *n.* An **obligation** is something you must do. *It is the boy's obligation to take care of the dog.*

optional *adj.* Something that is **optional** is not needed or required. *At our school, learning to play an instrument is an optional activity that you can choose.*

overcome *v.* To **overcome** something is to succeed at something that is difficult. *If you used to be afraid of dogs but now you like them, you have overcome your fear.*

P

parasite *n.* A **parasite** is an organism that gets food or shelter from living in or on another organism. *The fleas on the dog were parasites.*

participate *v.* When you **participate**, you do something with others. *The students participate on a sports team.*

peer *v.* To **peer** means to look at something closely. *The archaeologists peered into the tomb to see the treasure.*

perspective *n.* A **perspective** is a point of view. *The students discussed their different perspectives about the issues.*

pharaoh *n.* A **pharaoh** is a ruler of ancient Egypt. *Ramses II is often called the greatest pharaoh of ancient Egypt.*

plunder *v.* To **plunder** means to take something by force. *The robbers plundered the tomb and left nothing but broken jars behind them.*

policy *n.* A **policy** is an official guide to how something should be done. *They followed the policy to keep their school clean.*

potential *n.* **Potential** is the ability to change or improve in the future. *The kids have potential to become great basketball players one day.*

powerful *adj.* A **powerful** person has the ability to control other people or things. *The powerful judge makes decisions in a courtroom.*

preservation *n.* **Preservation** means to keep something from being lost. *The preservation of culture is important, and that is why people celebrate certain holidays.*

procession *n.* A **procession** is when people move forward together during a ceremony or festival. *Ancient Egyptians held funeral processions when important people died.*

protection *n.* **Protection** keeps people, animals, and things safe. *Helmets give protection to the bikers' heads.*

R

recover *v.* **Recover** means to get something back. *She recovered her health after having the flu.*

regulate *v.* When something is **regulated**, it is controlled by rules, a law, or an authority figure. *They regulated how many people could enter the zoo so that it wouldn't become overcrowded.*

reliance *n.* **Reliance** is the condition of needing something or someone else for help or support. *All humans have a reliance on food.*

representation *n.* A **representation** is a picture or other image that stands for a person or thing. *The statue is a representation of an ancient Egyptian king.*

reputation *n.* A **reputation** is an overall quality or characteristic of a person that others notice. *She had the reputation of being the best at math in the class.*

resemblance *n.* When things share a **resemblance**, they look alike. *The twins share a strong resemblance because their features are very similar.*

resilience *n.* When you show **resilience**, you can recover from or adapt to difficult situations. *Plants show resilience by growing in places with little or no soil.*

Dictionary

resistance *n.* **Resistance** is the act of taking a stand against something. *The cat showed* ***resistance*** *when it refused to go outside.*

resolve *v.* When you **resolve** to do something, you reach a decision about it. *After seeing the litter, the kids* ***resolve*** *to pick up trash once a week.*

resourceful *adj.* To be **resourceful** means to be creative in finding new materials for your needs. *She was very* ***resourceful*** *when she used the old egg carton for her art project.*

reveal *v.* When you **reveal** something, you show or explain it to others. *The magician* ***reveals*** *the rabbit that was in his hat.*

S

sensitive *adj.* To be **sensitive** means to be aware of the feelings of others. *She had a* ***sensitive*** *nature and didn't like seeing anyone or anything in pain.*

significant *adj.* Something **significant** is important. *Finding King Tut's tomb was a* ***significant*** *discovery for archaeologists.*

sustain *v.* To **sustain** is to continue or keep up an action, event, or thing. *The runner drinks lots of water to* ***sustain*** *her during the race.*

T

thrive *v.* To **thrive** means to grow strong and healthy. *With lots of care, plants can* ***thrive***.

tolerance *n.* When you have **tolerance**, you understand and have respect for beliefs that are different from your own. *He showed* ***tolerance*** *when he took off his baseball cap during the ceremony.*

tomb *n.* A **tomb** is a grave, or a special place for the body of a dead person. *The discovery of King Tut's* ***tomb*** *was very important to historians and archaeologists.*

U

utilize *v.* When you **utilize** something, you use it to do a job. *The gardeners* ***utilize*** *a shovel to collect leaves.*

V

variation *n.* **Variation** is the extent to which a thing changes. *The temperature showed extreme* ***variation*** *when it snowed in the morning and was sunny in the afternoon.*

Index

A

Adaptations, animal 72, 73, 78–91, 95–101

Adjectives
see Conventions; Grammar

Adverbs
see Conventions; Grammar

Antonyms 56

Argument 220
make an **220, 221, 286–289**

Ask questions 180
of author 153, 191
of text **146**, 147, 163, 167, 181, 196, 201, 203
see also Speaking

Audience, writing for a particular 286

Author's purpose 283

Author's style 197, 275

Author's viewpoint 33, 99, 167, **222**, 231, 233, 235, 237, **243**, 249

B

Base words 166, **244**

Bibliography 211

C

Cause and effect 31, 150

Character
actions **106**
analyzing **123**
goal 274
motives **106**, 120
plot and **38, 55**
traits 207
viewpoint **254**, 263, 269, **277**

Chronological order 144, 155, **165**

Claims
evidence 287

Clarify 49, 85, 129

Compare
author's viewpoint **234**

characters **62**
choices **132**
details **208**
genres **284**
information **174**
main ideas **34**
texts **102**

Comparisons, making 53, 81

Compound words 200

Conclusions, drawing
see Synthesize

Confirm predictions 23, 29

Connections, making 129, 225, 249, **256**, 257, 263, 269, 274, 279, 283
text to self 27, 57, 125, 167, 201, **224**, 235, 239, 241, 245, 279
text to text 27, 57, 95, 125, 167, 201, **224**, 245
text to world 27, 95, 167, **224**, 229, 245, 279

Conventions
parts of speech
adjectives **133**, 197, **251**
adverbs 197, **251**
nouns 67
participial phrases **285**
pronouns **103, 133**
verbs **175**, 197, 209
sentences **35**, 121
subject-verb agreement **63**

D

Define and explain
see Speaking

Describe 72

Details 17, 87, 159, 229

Determine importance
identify main idea and details 6, **25**, **74**, 83, 89, **93**, 95
summarize 23, 83, 163, 171, 205

Dictionary 26
meanings 292–296

E

Egypt, ancient
archaeologists 147, 149–162, 162–173
excavation 142, 147, 149–162, 162–173
mummies 162–173

Environment
ecology 227–241, 245–249
endangered species 225, 233–241, 245–249
plant diversity 259–274
rainforest 245–249
redwoods 253, 279–283
Yellowstone National Park 236–241
sandalwood 257

Explain 29, 31, 85, 97, **142**, 153, 161, 169, 191, 201, 237, 241, 247, 281
see also Speaking

F

Facts
interpreting from graphics 226, 232

Figurative language
see Imagery

Fluency 25, 55, 93, 123, 165, 199, 243, 277

G

Generalizations
see Synthesize

Genre
adventure story **110**
argument **286**
biography **10, 57**
blog 257
diary **182**
environmental report **226**
essay 279
expository report **134**

Index of Authors

Index of Illustrators

Text and Illustrator Credits

Unit One

27–33 From The Moth, edited by Catherine Burns. Copyright © 2013 by The Moth. Copyright © 2013 by Aimee Mullins. Reprinted by permission of Hachette Books.

Unit Two

78–91 Deception: Formula for Survival by Robert F. Sisson, National Geographic Magazine, March 1980, Vol. 157, Issue 3, pages 394–415. Reprinted with permission of National Geographic Learning.

95–101 Living Nightmares by Lynn Brunelle, National Geographic Extreme Explorer, October 2013, pages 2–9.

110–121 From *HATCHET* by Gary Paulsen. Copyright © 1987 Gary Paulsen. Reprinted with the permission of Flannery Literary Agency and Atheneum Books for Young Readers, an imprint of Simon & Schuster Children's Publishing Division. All rights reserved.

125–131 From the book "When I Fell from the Sky" by Juliane Koepcke, published by The Reader's Digest Association in 2014. Reprinted with permission from Title Town Publishing.

Unit Three

148–163 Valley of the Kings by Dr. Kent Weeks, published by National Geographic Magazine, September 1998. Reprinted with permission from the author.

167–171, Animals Everlasting by A.R. Williams, National Geographic, November 2009. Reprinted with permission of National Geographic Learning.

201–207 Excerpt(s) from The Golden Goblet by Eloise Jarvis McGraw, copyright © 1961, renewed © 1989 by Eloise Jarvis McGraw. Used by permission of Puffin Books, an imprint of Penguin Young Readers Group, a division of Penguin Random House LLC. All rights reserved. Any third party use of this material, outside of this publication, is prohibited. Interested parties must apply directly to Penguin Random House LLC for permission.

245–249 Mireya Mayor by Mireya Mayor, National Geographic Society, Copyright 2014.

Unit Four

279–283 The Super Trees by Joel Bourne, National Geographic Society, October 2009. Reprinted with permission of National Geographic Learning.

Photographic Credits

Cover Keren Su/Getty Images. iii (tl) Francisco Negroni. (tr) Roy Toft/National Geographic Image Collection. (bl) Danita Delimont/Alamy Stock Photo. (br) G.M.B. Akash/Panos Pictures. 2–3 Francisco Negroni. 4 dmbaker/Getty Images. 5 (t) Wavebreak Media ltd/Alamy Stock Photo. (b) Viacheslav Iakobchuk/Alamy Stock Photo. 7 (tl) Janine Wiedel Photolibrary/Alamy Stock Photo. (tc) James Wheeler/Shutterstock.com. (tr) Margaret M Stewart/Shutterstock.com. (bl) Blend Images- KidStock/Brand X Pictures/Getty Images. (bc) Rebecca Nelson/Getty Images. 9 Frederic REGLAIN/Getty Images. 10–11 Dinodia Photos/Alamy Stock Photo. 12–13 Eye Ubiquitous/Getty Images. 13 (inset) Apic/RETIRED/Getty Images. 14 John van Hasselt - Corbis/Getty Images. 15 API/Getty Images. 16 age fotostock/Alamy Stock Photo.

17 Universal History Archive/Getty Images. 18 Keystone-France/Getty Images. (inset) Lordprice Collection/Alamy Stock Photo. 20–21 ullstein bild/Getty Images. 22 picture alliance/Getty Images. 23 Bettmann/Getty Images. 27 Photo courtesy of L'Oréal Paris. 28 Image by Catherine MacBride/Moment/Getty Images. 30 Solve Sundsbo/Art and Commerce. 31 LYNN JOHNSON/National Geographic Image Collection. 32 Rob Kim/Getty Images. 33 joshlaverty/iStock/Getty Images. 36 asiseeit/Getty Images. 37 (l) Evgeny Bakharev/Shutterstock.com. (r) Hero Images/Getty Images. 39 (tl) Andersen Ross/Blend Images/Getty Images. (tc) Echo/Juice Images/Getty Images. (tr) Christine Schneider/Brigitte Sporrer/Cultura/Getty Images. (bl) Myrleen Pearson/Alamy Stock Photo. (bc) Tim Clayton - Corbis/Corbis Sport/Getty Images. 41 Caiaimage/Sam Edwards/Getty Images. 57 Sheridan Libraries/Levy/Gado/Getty Images. 58 George Marks/Getty Images. 59 Bill Ray/Getty Images. 60 Bettmann/Getty Images. 61 Photo 12/Alamy Stock Photo. 67 Just dance/Shutterstock.com. 68 Francisco Negroni. 69 (l) Brooke Becker/Shutterstock.com. (r) Brian Jackson/Alamy Stock Photo. 70–71 Roy Toft/National Geographic Image Collection. 72 Pete Oxford/Nature Picture Library. 73 (butterfly-l) JASON EDWARDS/National Geographic Image Collection. (butterfly-r) David R. Frazier Photolibrary, Inc./Alamy Stock Photo. (snake-l) Design Pics/Jack Goldfarb/Getty Images. (snake-r) Dr. Morley Read/Shutterstock.co. (robber fly-l) Erhard Nerger/imageBROKER/Getty Images. (robber fly-r) Robert Servrancky/Visuals Unlimited, Inc. (owl) Rolf Nussbaumer/Nature Picture Library. (tick) ironman100 /iStock/Getty Images. 75 (tl) Cultura RM Exclusive/Ross Woodhall/Cultura Exclusive/Getty Images. (tc) Jupiterimages/PHOTOS.com/Getty Images. (tr) Andrii Ospishchev/Shutterstock.com. (bl) lola1960/Shutterstock.com. (bc) Wendy Connett/Moment Open/Getty Images. 78 ROBERT SISSON/National Geographic Image Collection. 78–79 Solvin Zankl/Visuals Unlimited, Inc./Getty Images. 80 ROBERT SISSON/National Geographic Image Collection. 81 (both) ROBERT SISSON/National Geographic Image Collection. 82 ROBERT SISSON/National Geographic Image Collection. 82–83 ROBERT SISSON/National Geographic Image Collection. 84 (both) ROBERT SISSON/National Geographic Image Collection. 85 (all) ROBERT SISSON/National Geographic Image Collection. 86 ROBERT E. HYNES /National Geographic Image Collection. 87 (all) ROBERT E. HYNES /National Geographic Image Collection. 88 (l) ROBERT SISSON/National Geographic Image Collection. (r) CARRIE VONDERHAAR/OCEAN FUTURES SOCIETY/National Geographic Image Collection. 89 ROBERT SISSON/National Geographic Image Collection. 90 (l) ROBERT SISSON/National Geographic Image Collection. (r) John Cancalosi/Alamy Stock Photo. (cr) Martin Shields/Alamy Stock Photo. (br) Thailand Wildlife/Alamy Stock Photo. 91 ROBERT SISSON/National Geographic Image Collection. 92 jps/Shutterstock.com. 95 Lillac /Shutterstock.com. 96 PAUL NICKLEN/National Geographic Image Collection. 97 Pete Oxford/Nature Picture Library. 98 Piotr Naskrecki/Minden Pictures/Getty Images. 99 F. Hecker/Blickwinkel/AGE Fotostock. 100 (tl) Dave Watts/Alamy Stock Photo. (br) Mitsuaki Iwago/Minden Pictures/Getty Images. 101 FLPA/Malcolm Schuyl/AGE Fotostock. 104 Dmitriy Shironosov/Alamy Stock Photo. (inset-l) Ed Freeman/Stone/Getty Images. (inset-r) Luca Deravignone/Moment Open/Getty Images. 107 (tl) Image Source/Zero Creatives/Getty Images. (tc) Danita Delimont/Alamy Stock Photo. (tr) JGI/Jamie Grill/Blend Images/Getty Images. (bl) Vast Photography/First Light/Getty Images. (br) Jim Parkin/Alamy Stock Photo. 121 Brian Adams/Getty Images. 125 Cyril Ruoso/Minden Pictures. (inset) Courtesy of Reader's Digest. 127 (t) Piotr Naskrecki/Minden Pictures. (b) schankz/Shutterstock.com.

128 (t) Milaspage/Shutterstock.com. (b) CORDIER Sylvain/hemis.fr/Getty Images. 129 (t) Madlen/Shutterstock.com. (b) Patricio Robles Gil/Minden Pictures. 130 g01xm/E+/Getty Images. 131 Perszing1982/iStock/Getty Images. 137 Dave Watts/Alamy Stock Photo. 138 Roy Toft/National Geographic Image Collection. 139 (tl) Manoj Shah/Oxford Scientific/Getty Images. (bl) Yuji Sakai/DigitalVision/Getty Images. (br) Marxon/Shutterstock.com. 140–141 Danita Delimont/Alamy Stock Photo. 142 (t) Sisse Brimberg/National Geographic Image Collection. (b) Fuse/Corbis/Getty Images. 143 (t) DEA PICTURE LIBRARY/De Agostini Picture Library/Getty Images. (c) Pool AVENTURIER/ROSSI/CNRS/Gamma-Rapho/Getty Images. (bl) Gianni Dagli Orti/Shutterstock.com, Erich Lessing/Art Resource, NY. 145 (tl) jperagine/Masterfile. (tc) Alistair Flack/Alamy Stock Photo. (tr) moodboard/Brand X Pictures/Getty Images. (bl) Robert Harding/robertharding/Getty Images. (bc) ClassicStock/Alamy Stock Photo. 147 Barry Iverson/The LIFE Images Collection/Getty Images. 148–149 Ed Giles/Getty Images News/Getty Images 151 (tl) Heritage Images/Hulton Archive/Getty Images. (cl) Head and upper torso of Seti I, New Kingdom 1303-1200 B.C. (granite), Egyptian 19th Dynasty (c.1297-1185 BC)/Dallas Museum of Art, Texas, USA/Bridgeman Images. (cr) DEA PICTURE LIBRARY/De Agostini Picture Library/Getty Images. (b) S. VANNINI/Contributor/Getty Images. (br) Egypt - Ancient Thebes (UNESCO World Heritage List, 1979). Valley of the Kings. Funerary temple of Ramses II 'Ramesseum'. Figures of Osiris at inner court pillars/De Agostini Picture Library/S. Vannini/Bridgeman Images. 153 Kenneth Garrett/National Geographic Image Collection. 154 Kenneth Garrett/National Geographic Image Collection. 157 Barry Iverson/The LIFE Images Collection/Getty Images. 158 Kenneth Garrett/National Geographic Image Collection. 160 Danita Delimont/Gallo Images/Getty Images. 161 Kenneth Garrett/National Geographic Image Collection. 162 Kenneth Garrett/National Geographic Image Collection. 163 DEA/G. DAGLI ORTI/De Agostini/Getty Images. 164 Kenneth Garrett/National Geographic Image Collection. 167 Erich Lessing/Art Resource, NY. 168 Richard Barnes. 170–171 De Agostini/S. Vannini/Getty Images. 173 (l) DEA PICTURE LIBRARY/De Agostini/Getty Images. (cl) DEA/G. DAGLI ORTI/Getty Images. (cr) Kenneth Garrett/National Geographic Image Collection. (r) JoseIgnacioSoto/iStock/Getty Images. 176 PKS Media Inc/SuperStock. 179 (tl) Tom Burlison/Shutterstock.com. (tc) Adrian Sherratt/Alamy Stock Photo. (tr) Peter Muller/Cultura/Getty Images. (bl) Florian Kopp/ imageBROKER/Alamy Stock Photo. (bc) mountainpix/Shutterstock.com. 196 Heritage Image Partnership Ltd/Alamy Stock Photo. 197 Laura Meza. 216 Danita Delimont/Alamy Stock Photo. 217 PHAS/Universal Images Group/Getty Images. 218–219 G.M.B. Akash/Panos Pictures. 220 (l) Photodisc/Getty Images. (r) Eric Baccega/Grey wolf/Canis lupus/Nature Picture Library. 221 (t) BRIAN J. SKERRY/National Geographic Image Collection. (c) Bloomberg/Getty Images. (b) Barry Bland/Nature Picture Library. 223 (tl) ZouZou/Shutterstock.com. (tc) Bounce/Cultura/Getty Images. (tr) Comstock/Stockbyte/Getty Images. (bl) Ariel Skelley/DigitalVision/Getty Images. (bc) Michaelpuche/Shutterstock.com. 225 (t) stephan kerkhofs/Shutterstock.com. (b) Radharc Images/Alamy Stock Photo. 226–227 Michele Westmorland/Corbis Documentary/Getty Images. 228 Pete Oxford/ Minden Pictures/Getty Images. 229 SKIP BROWN/National Geographic Image Collection. 230 John Mock/Lonely Planet Images/Getty Images. 233 (bkgd) BRIAN J. SKERRY/National Geographic Image Collection. (tr) DENIS-HUOT/hemis.fr/Getty Images. (cr) Joel Sartore/National Geographic Image Collection. (br) Martin Willis/ Minden Pictures/Getty Images. 234 (l) CHRIS JOHNS/National Geographic Image

Acknowledgments

The Authors and Publisher would like to thank the following reviewers and teaching professionals for their valuable feedback during the development of the series.

Literature Reviewers

Carmen Agra Deedy, Grace Lin, Jonda C. McNair, Anastasia Suen

Global Reviewers

USA/Canada:

Terrie Armstrong, Bilingual/ESL Program Team Leader, Houston Independent School District, Houston, TX; **Irma Bravo Lawrence,** Director II, District and Englisher Learner, Support Services, Stanislaus County Office of Education, Turlock, CA; **Julie Folkert,** Language Arts Coordinator, Farmington Public Schools, Farmington, MI; **Norma Godina-Silva,** Ph. D, Bilingual Education/ESL/Title III Consultant, ESL-BilingualResources.com, El Paso, TX; **Keely Krueger,** Director of Bilingual Education, Woodstock Community Unit School 200, Woodstock, IL; **Myra Junyk,** Literacy Consultant, Toronto, ON; **Lore Levene,** Coordinator of Language Arts, NBCT Community Consolidated School, District 59, Mt. Prospet, IL; **Estee Lopez,** Professor of Literacy Education and ELL Specialist, College of New Rochelle, New Rochelle, NY; **Christine Kay Williams,** ESOL Teacher, Baltimore County Public Schools, Baltimore, MD.

Asia:

Mohan Aiyer, School Principal, Brainworks International School, Yangon; **Andrew Chuang,** Weige Primary School, Taipei; **Sherefa Dickson,** Head Teacher, SMIC, Beijing; **Ms Hien,** IP Manager, IPS Vietnam, Ho Chi Minh; **Christine Huang,** Principal, The International Bilingual School at the Hsinchu Science Park (IBSH), Hsinchu; **Julie Hwang,** Academic Consultant, Seoul; **David Kwok,** CEO, Englit Enterprise, Guangzhou; **Emily Li,** Teaching Assistant, SMIC, Beijing; **Warren Martin,** English Teacher, Houhai English, Beijing; **Bongse Memba,** Academic Coordinator, SMIC, Beijing; **Hoai Minh Nguyen,** Wellspring International Bilingual School, Ho Chi Minh; **Mark Robertson,** Elementary School Principal, Yangon Academy, Yangon; **Daphne Tseng,** American Eagle Institute, Hsinchu; **Amanda Xu,** Director of Teaching and Research, Englit Enterprise, Guangzhou; **Alice Yamamoto,** ALT, PL Gakuen Elementary School, Osaka; **Yan Yang,** Director of Research Development, Houhai English, Beijing

Middle East:

Lisa Olsen, Teacher, GEMS World Academy, Dubai, United Arab Emirates; **Erin Witthoft,** Curriculum Coordinator, Universal American School, Kuwait

Latin America:

Federico Brull, Academic Director, Cambridge School of Monterrey, Mexico; **Elizabeth Caballero,** English Coordinator, Ramiro Kolbe Campus Otay, Mexico; **Renata Callipo,** Teacher, CEI Romualdo, Brazil; **Lilia Huerta,** General Supervisor, Ramiro Kolbe Campus Presidentes, Mexico; **Rosalba Millán,** English Coordinator Primary, Instituto Cenca, Mexico; **Ann Marie Moreira,** Academic Consultant, Brazil; **Raúl Rivera,** English Coordinator, Ramiro Kolbe Campus Santa Fe, Mexico; **Leonardo Xavier,** Teacher, CEI Romualdo, Brazil

The Publisher gratefully acknowledges the contributions of the following National Geographic Explorers to our program and planet:

Kent Weeks, Salima Ikram, Mireya Mayor, and Mike Fay